When the Sun Bursts

When the Sun Bursts

The Enigma of Schizophrenia

CHRISTOPHER BOLLAS

Yale

UNIVERSITY PRESS

New Haven & London

Yale University Press books may be purchased in quantity for educational,
business, or promotional use. For information, please e-mail
sales.press@yale.edu (U.S. office) or sales@yaleup.co.uk (U.K. office).

Set in Fournier type by IDS Infotech, Ltd.
Printed in the United States of America.

Library of Congress Control Number: 2015938095
ISBN 978-0-300-21473-4 (cloth : alk. paper)

A catalogue record for this book is available from the British Library.

This paper meets the requirements of ANSI/NISO Z39.48-1992
(Permanence of Paper).

10 9 8 7 6 5 4 3 2 1

Contents

Contents

Acknowledgments

THERE ARE MANY PEOPLE to thank for making this book possible, especially if I think back to what I learned from teachers, supervisors, and colleagues over the decades. It does not feel right to simply list them, but I owe a great deal to those analysts in Great Britain who always assumed that schizophrenic people were analyzable.

I owe a special debt to the various institutions where I worked with psychotic people: the East Bay Activity Center (EBAC) in Oakland, California, the Department of Psychiatry of Beth Israel Hospital in Boston, the Personal Consultation Centre in London, and the Austen Riggs Center in Stockbridge, Massachusetts. I am grateful for the times when I supervised staff members or trainees at the Arbours Association (London) and the Philadelphia Association (London). Twenty years of teaching and supervising at the Istituto di Neuro-psichiatria Infantile of the University of Rome allowed me to follow in-patient treatment of many psychotic children and adolescents over the years. I am grateful for my spell as a visiting scholar at the Menninger Clinic in Topeka.

I would not have been able to undertake work of this kind on an outpatient basis without the help of a remarkably skilled group of people. One of these, whom I am calling "Dr. Branch," was a general practitioner and psychiatrist in London who provided "medical coverage" for most of my psychotic patients. In addition I had the help—in the 1970s—of the local area team of social workers, as well as family members and friends of my patients who sustained them through hard times. Some of my schizophrenic patients had been hospitalized, but thanks to the expertise of the team, none had to return to hospital either on our watch or afterward. I have discussed this patient-team approach in another work, on acute breakdown in non-psychotic people (*Catch Them Before They Fall: The Psychoanalysis of Mental Breakdown*), but the team also functioned to help me with people who otherwise would have had to be in either residential care or hospital treatment.

I am grateful to Sarah Nettleton for her astute comments and the thought and care provided through editing the work. I thank Molly McDonald for her editorial help. I thank my literary editor, Leslie Gardner, for her commitment to this book, for her endless patience and her wisdom. I am grateful to Jennifer Banks, Executive Editor of Yale University Press, for her support and her thoughtful discussions of the differing issues that arose along the way.

I also thank two young Finnish psychologists and psychoanalytical psychotherapists, Teija Nissinen and Antto Luhtavaara, who maintain the remarkable tradition in Finland of resolute belief that a schizophrenic is best helped through intensive psychotherapy, and who read the first and last drafts of this work and provided frank and astute critiques.

I thank the Chicago Workshop in Psychoanalysis for discussing many of the ideas presented in the first decade of this century. I also thank "Keeping Our Work Alive" and its coordinator, Bill Cornell, in Pittsburgh for a weekend devoted to presenting the clinical ideas in the book. Special thanks to the Los Angeles Institute and Society for Psychoanalytic Study (LAISPS) for their one-day conference on this topic where I gained valued responses.

For thirty years I met each summer in Arild (Sweden) with twenty-five Swedish analysts and psychotherapists, organized and chaired by Ulla Bejerholm. All of the ideas in this book were put before that group over the years, and I shall be forever grateful for their gracious and intelligent responses.

Note to the Reader

THIS WORK TRACES THE DEVELOPMENT of my understanding of how to work with schizophrenic people, and I include many accounts from teachers, supervisors, colleagues, and friends. The relevant historical facts are included, but otherwise descriptions of the patients and their histories are fictionalized for purposes of confidentiality. Each one represents a real person I worked with, however, and the conversations reported are not disguised. The clinical vignettes are accurate and are provided because they teach us something about the psychotic and schizophrenic process. I hope that the psychological and emotional truths of these relationships will be conveyed to the reader.

When the Sun Bursts

Introduction

WHEN I WAS AN UNDERGRADUATE at the University of California in the mid-1960s, I was caught up in the passions of the Free
Speech Movement, then the anti-war movement, and then by chance
the Black Panther Party. At the same time I was studying history and
was rather immersed in the early seventeenth century, following the
lives of several Puritan miscreants in the villages that were to become
Boston.

In the hubbub, I developed symptoms. To my bewilderment, I was
suddenly afraid of heights and especially stairwells. Although I was
not in the least consciously suicidal, I had a thought that I might
impulsively leap to my death. Before long I was sitting in the office of
a psychoanalyst at the university health center.

I ended up in weekly psychotherapy for two years, and it changed
my life. Through the curious pathways to self-discovery invented by
Freud, and especially through free association, the meanings of the
symptoms were revealed, and to my surprise they had nothing at all
to do with their manifest content. What a mystery the mind was. During my therapy I began reading psychoanalysis and discovered a rich
storehouse of found truths and, more important, ways of perceiving

unconscious reality that opened up a new vista for me. I applied those perspectives to my senior thesis on the psychological conflicts of seventeenth-century New England Puritans, and from that moment on psychoanalysis became a part of my intellectual life.

Although over time I read Freud and most of the classical psychoanalytic texts, I felt a rift between the experience and the literature, and I turned to clinical work rather than to psychoanalytical studies to follow the fascinating project named psychoanalysis.

Psychoanalysis is a twentieth-century development: a new position to observe and comment on the vicissitudes of human being. In the course of a career it is the analyst's privilege to encounter many fascinating people and to share in the work of self-examination that so often proves personally transformative.

No one a psychoanalyst meets is more compelling than the schizophrenic.

By chance, I began my career with autistic and schizophrenic children. I knew from the beginning, however, that to work with a schizophrenic was to study the enigma of being human and the potential to lose one's mind.

I shall follow my career in a chronological order. I focus on what I learned from my own clinical experience, although my perceptions were influenced by seminars and supervisions during my years of training. The views expressed here therefore reflect in differing ways the teachings of, among others, Wilfred Bion, R. D. Laing, Hanna Segal, Betty Joseph, Herbert Rosenfeld, Henri Rey, Leslie Sohn, and John Steiner.

No one could possibly be an expert in the field of mental health. Any of us working with people are only as effective as students. Of course we have been book-educated and taken seminars and been in supervision, but no human life is long enough to allow any clinician to claim that he or she has truly grasped the meaning of any of the "disorders," whether it be manic depression, paranoia, or schizophrenia. What we can do, however, is to pass on what we think we have learned, and it is in that spirit that this project was undertaken.

Most people I know who have talked with schizophrenics have noticed that these feel like conversations not with someone whose ailment is derived from the fog of symptomatic preoccupation, or the dulling repetition of character patterns, but with a person who seems to be existing on the edge of human perception. Take LSD and you see things you would ordinarily never perceive. Become schizophrenic and you see these things without the aid of drugs.

In other words, schizophrenia is puzzling.

This work is not a textbook. It does not present the vast literature on the topic, nor does it address the countless issues surrounding it: from theories of where it originates to the many differing views of how it should be treated. (And I do not discuss either Freud's major contributions or those of his contemporaries, such as Paul Federn.) Some of the major works on schizophrenia in English, however, can be found in the Annotated Bibliography. For those interested in present-day clinical research in schizophrenia I recommend the International Society for Psychological and Social Approaches to Psychosis (formerly the International Society for the Psychological Treatments of the Schizophrenias and Other Psychoses), at www.isps. org. Routledge is publishing an impressive series of books sponsored by the ISPS, edited by Brian Martindale, that will bring contemporary readers up to speed with revitalized interest in the psychotherapy of the schizophrenic.

This book follows from a recent companion volume, *Catch Them Before They Fall: The Psychoanalysis of Breakdown* (2013). Some of the themes concerning treatment of acute psychic situations are quite similar, especially the need to assemble a team of professionals to help the psychoanalyst work with the patient.

I have refrained from discussing the possible causes of schizophrenia. I do not know the answer to this. To me it is rather like asking what causes the being of human being. Nonetheless a certain theme emerges in this book, one that I was already arguing in my book *Being a Character:* to be a child is to endure a prolonged situation in which the human mind is more complex than the self can ordinarily bear. However puzzling the circumstances in our world, however disturbing our parents and others may be, our minds—in themselves—produce contents that will be overwhelming. To be successfully normal, then, we rather have to dumb ourselves down.

Work with schizophrenics has taught me that when defenses against the complexities of mind break down there can be a breakthrough of too much. Selves cave in. Many recover, usually by means of a collective human inclination to group together through alliances that simplify one's being: marriage, work-life, raising a family. The schizophrenic position is one where a self's embedment in the solace of the quotidian is breached, and consciousness is confronted with both the complexities of thought processes and the raw materials of unconscious function.

I do not discuss differential diagnoses among the schizophrenias. When writing about my work with children I adhere to a phenomenological distinction used in the 1960s: an autistic child did not speak or engage the other visually. A schizophrenic child was verbal and engaging but perceived reality through psychotic lenses. Some autistic children, such as my patient Nick, did emerge into speech and relational engagements. In those days the child would still have a diagnosis of autism because, unlike the schizophrenic child, he or she could perceive reality in a non-psychotic way. The autistic self could emerge, by adolescence and young adulthood, substantially better off mentally and relationally than those children who were diagnosed as schizophrenics.

I also do not aim to provide "outcome studies." How successful have I been in working with schizophrenic people? What do I observe about how efficacious psychoanalysis is when other clinicians use it? I wish I could answer these questions in depth, but I cannot. The simple fact is that for the most part after an analysis is concluded I do not see my analysands again. I do not ask them to keep me informed about how they are getting on, and few of my former patients stay in touch.

I shall concentrate, instead, on a few key aspects of the schizo-phrenic process that I have found to have intriguing relevance to understanding the wider picture.

What does a schizophrenic person look like after what I consider to be a successful analysis? There is no ready answer to this any more than there is to the question frequently posed to non-psychotic analy-sands: "What did you get out of your analysis?" Schizophrenics vary in their own idioms as much as non-schizophrenic people, but I con-sider it a successful analysis if the person has turned away from hallucinations and psychotic defenses, relates and functions in non-psychotic ways, and is no longer suffering the mental pain of being schizophrenic. I do not think a person who has had a schizophrenic breakdown will ever forget it, nor do I think anyone is ever entirely free of it, any more than a person can recover from childhood to the point of no longer recollecting it or being influenced by it. However, I shall quote one schizophrenic who, some fifteen years after his last schizophrenic episode (hearing voices, intense paranoid withdrawal, speechlessness), said, "Well, I was schizophrenic and now I think I am just schizoid."

Although I may not be able to provide the sort of backup for my assertions that some readers would want, the evidence, such as it is, is in the writing. I have provided samples of the way I think about schizophrenics and how I work with them, and I hope I have offered a clear picture of the many differing idioms of working with schizophrenic people. The reader will come to his or her own conclusions about the merits of my approach. My aim is to nudge us into rethinking schizophrenia.

It may be useful to draw a distinction between arguments that are based in the humanities or the sciences. Carl Schorske, who taught intellectual history at the University of California, said that in the humanities universal conclusions are often drawn from the detailed examination of a single work. The sciences approach the epistemological in a different way. Scientists claim a universal truth only by casting a wide net to search for very particular phenomena that can be cross-checked by other scientists.

Freud came to complex universal assumptions about the mind through studying single case histories. Similarly, scholars of the humanities would argue that a single work of drama—*Hamlet*—has taught us more about mental conflict than any number of scientific studies on mental life. Scientific evidence and scholarly evidence are not the same, even if the word is used in both realms. Scholars are judged through the credibility of their arguments, which of course include their use of primary source material. Hundreds of essays have been written about schizophrenia and also about *Hamlet*. New "evidence" in the examination of *Hamlet* will ordinarily come from a new way of looking at the play, an interpretation of the text not previously entertained, that evokes in the reader the experience of learning something quite new about the play or human psychology.

For almost a hundred years many psychiatrists, psychologists, and psychoanalysts have cooperated in the treatment of schizophrenic people. Although some members of these professions remained insulated by adhering to a generically hostile attitude toward the other approaches, for the most part hospitals, clinics, and their offshoots in private practice created fruitful cooperation between the professions.

However, one need not be a mental health professional to be aware of an intense campaign by some branches of modern psychiatry and psychopharmacology to assert that schizophrenia is genetically determined—to be treated only through a combination of maintenance medication and occasional periods of hospitalization. Any meaningful research, in this view, must be in the direction of finding the perfect medication for each of the strands of schizophrenia.

The quest for a biological solution to the problems posed by serious mental disturbance has attracted all the professions, including psychoanalysis. Freud believed that eventually a biological solution would be found for all of the mental conditions, thus rendering psychoanalysis unnecessary.

While I do not share that view, it is important for readers of this book to know that even if few of my schizophrenic patients were on medication, sleeping medications were occasionally valuable. So too were benzodiazepine on an "as needed" basis. Many people find it reassuring to have a Valium in their pocket just in case events in the real prove too disturbing.

None of these alternative treatments were as helpful, however, as body therapies, such as daily massage, which was hugely helpful in working with my patients when they could tolerate it.

Sadly, many of today's hospitalized schizophrenics are receiving powerful anti-psychotic medications, and being discharged on a cocktail of drugs that dulls their lives. Their zombie-like states are caused not so much by their mental alterity as by the results of medication.

No doubt there are follow-up studies of formerly hospitalized schizophrenics showing that long-term maintenance medications and repeated hospitalization have proved effective. Certain behavioral modifications would be noticeable and evident. However, the community of doctors, psychiatrists, psychologists, psychopharmacologists and others who ply the trade of the pharmaceutical complex in the "maintenance" and control of schizophrenia may fail to ask the question: at what cost?

One of the tragedies of the schizophrenic fate in the past and in the present is the "throw the key away" finality of those who deem themselves experts in this area. Whereas in the past, patients were simply locked away in hospitals where many would remain for a lifetime, today they are more likely to suffer psychotropic incarceration. The necessity is to find some way to get rid of their symptoms. That the symptom and the person are in many respects one and the same, and that medication can threaten to eradicate the human dimension, is too often disregarded.

People with schizophrenia may need to be in hospital, or to take some form of medication in order to help rediscover the useful parts of the mind. However, I am also aware of successful work with schizophrenics in which no medication has been administered and the analysand has never been in hospital. I am by no means the only psychoanalyst who has worked with some schizophrenics without medication, but I am not in a position to argue that this would be possible in all cases.

In my view, the more crucial issue is to distinguish between a treatment approach that is "generative" and one that is not.

There is one thing at the beginning of schizophrenia—one crucial factor—that is vital to whether the person has a chance to survive and reverse the process. It is crucial that there is someone for the person to talk to for long periods of time, perhaps several times a day, for days and possibly weeks.

Some—sadly a very few—hospitals do offer something approaching this sort of care by assigning a primary therapist who can work intensively with the patient. But antipathy in psychiatry and psychopharmacology to the so-called "talking therapies" means that too often schizophrenics are left in relational isolation except for occasional short visits with a psychiatrist.

The tragic irony of this approach is that the patient is then met with a process parallel to schizophrenia itself: radical incarceration, mind-altering actions, dehumanization, isolation.

It does not need to be this way. But we now live in an era where the mind is tending to be viewed as merely synonymous with the brain. In fact, the idea that mental problems can be solved through neurological intervention is a category error as ridiculous as confusing a radio program with the radio itself. If we are to provide a humane route for the schizophrenic person then we need to offer immediate, intensive, and open-ended psychotherapy.

We all know the wisdom of talking. In trouble, we turn to an other. Being listened to inevitably generates new perspective, and the help we get lies not only in what is said but in that human connection intrinsic to the therapeutic process of talking that promotes unconscious thinking.

When we are in trouble, talking to an empathic other is curative.

We all know that. We all do it. And we do not need outcome studies to prove to us that it works. And yet it is precisely this ancient means of helping the self through its roughest mental and existential quandaries that is so often denied to the schizophrenic person.

If intensive psychotherapy is provided in the first weeks of a person's schizophrenic onset, there is a good chance that clinicians will see transformations back to non-psychotic functioning.

Intensive therapy works.

It is especially effective in reversing the beginnings of schizophrenia, as this is almost inevitably an event in adolescence. Like the anorectic, the schizophrenic fails to make the transition from childhood to adulthood: something goes wrong. But precisely because selves falter during this period, they can also turn around and rediscover an ordinary track to life. So although they are highly vulnerable to all kinds of disturbances, this porosity also makes them uniquely open to therapeutic change.

Throughout this text I contrast schizophrenics with "normals." Objectionable as this may seem, I use the distinction because it is exactly the way schizophrenics experience themselves and the life they live. They know they are not normal and yearn for ordinary life. Different from all other people—their own radical visions pose a greater, and more generative, challenge to our norms than anyone else—their aim is to lose themselves in the bliss of the ordinary.

The book is divided into three parts. Part One is an account of my early years learning from schizophrenic children and adults. Part Two delves into the heart of theory—an effort to explain certain aspects of the way schizophrenics think and behave. Part Three discusses the psychotherapy of schizophrenia.

The challenge of working with the schizophrenic remains, to my mind, a portal to further study of the human being. Perhaps it is to our time what the dream was to Freud. In that respect this work is written for any reader interested in depth psychology and the more vexing mysteries of human being.

This book is dedicated to my schizophrenic patients, to their brilliantly inventive solutions to their predicament and especially to their profound courage.

PART ONE

I

Up Against the Wall

IN THE 1960S THE EAST BAY Activity Center clung to a hillside in Oakland, California, just a few hundred yards below the towering sphinx of a Mormon temple, its fading green structures weathered by the relentless sea-driven winds of the Bay Area. As the kids passed through the front gate, the workshop was to their left, the classrooms and administrative offices to their right. In front of them was a wide pathway to the playing fields, from which they could see in the distance the glistening shocking white of San Francisco—commemorative icon of the power and success of the westward movement.

Whether they were running on to the field for the joy of it or dashing there to escape some pursuing demon, occasionally the panorama beyond caught them by surprise, a startling vision of what could be possible for them. Objectifying a world so far away, it stood out like a utopia few would ever reach.

The school day began around nine in the morning and ended around two in the afternoon. The kids, who ranged in age from five to twelve, were all assigned a "primary therapist" or "counselor," but all the staff and children knew one another. There were about thirty children, seven full-time staff members, and a lot of part-timers (usually students from the University of California at Berkeley) who provided extra cover for the children. I was twenty-three and just graduated from Berkeley, with a degree in history. I was thrown in at the "deep end" of the clinical world, working with psychotic children for two years, a baptism of profound and lasting consequence.

Each day began with the same routine.

Most of the staff members would stand on the school side of the large front gate where parents dropped their children off and would watch for the child we'd been assigned. Each one would pass through the entryway differently. Anthony would cling to the outside of the fence and his therapist would talk to him through the chain links and eventually coax him into crossing the invisible line into the school grounds. Tommy would stand at the entrance. If he felt okay he would do a kind of visual surveillance, as if inspecting the institution in preparation for making some kind of report. If he was not okay he would rock his clenched fist back and forth in a tick-tock motion accompanied by a whirring sound and then he would run into the field and disappear around the corner. His therapist always said, "Hi there, Tommy," standing to the side so that Tommy could run past him into the field. It would take some minutes for the clocklike motion to slow down and for Tommy to move into language.

I was assigned to a young Polish kid named Nick. Like all of the therapists, I learned it was important to watch how he climbed out of his car, because then I could sense what sort of morning we were likely to have. If he emerged with a tight smile on his face, eyes blinking, I knew that upon crossing the threshold he would rush up, kick me in the shins, spit on me, and then immediately try to attack a nearby child, unless I restrained his elbows. I would then escort him to the field, turn quickly to the right, drop to the ground against "our wall" and hold him with my arms.

Once seated, he would stop resisting. He would talk and talk and talk about who he was going to beat up, and why, and how I could not stop him.

Other times, if he got out of the car without the tight smile and blinking eyes, but shaking his hands, I knew that he would turn left upon entry and try to run into the school to attack the shop teacher, who was well accustomed to Nick's run-by thumpings. Some days he would leave the car with a furrowed brow, looking about him, turning around several times. Then I knew he was terrified and needed me to take him into the school building as soon as possible. There we would tuck his lunch box into its special place and he would need to find Larry.

Larry was a remarkable child. He was unusually tall for a ten-year-old and had long blond hair that went in all sorts of directions, adding to a mercurial atmosphere he seemed to generate. He kept up an ongoing comic-book version of life in the school. In the morning he would come up to someone who was due to be transformed into a comic-book figure that day, lick his forefinger and gently touch them on the forehead. It was like a religious moment, and I never saw any child try to get out of his way. They knew he had cast a spell on them and they would soon find out what he had in store. He would say: "This is the fickle finger of fate!"

So Nick would know that Larry would either have bestowed a good day upon him, or he would have fated him to be sent into some horrible situation. If it was the latter, then the question was whether Nick could survive staying at the center through the day.

The therapists at EBAC would take time to decipher the encrypted signs of the children's states of mind. It was not easy to do this, but it was not impossible. It meant reading their body language, learning how simple gestures were part of individual sign systems, and then finding some way to translate body thought into language in order to help them through their particular fears. The point was to catch them before they fell to pieces, because if that happened they would usually have to go back home right away. We all got a lot of things wrong. They were very different from one another, just like the rest of us, and there were no ready-made ways to be with them. Their reactions to the world were their way of telling us who they were.

Working with Nick, I came to understand what the psychoanalyst Victor Tausk wrote about as the schizophrenic's "influencing machine."[1] Nick would say, "I have to put the pegs right." He would tell me about the pendulum he had in his bedroom that would swing back and forth following a clockwise motion. If it was working well it would complete its daily circuit without incident. If it was not working it would knock over a domino, which meant to Nick that things were out of control.

A few times, when Nick was falling to pieces, we would have to call his parents so they could fetch him and take him home to his "pendulum," so he could recover. He and his parents would speak briefly in Polish on the phone, and in a matter of minutes a car would show up at the school and Nick would jump in.

More often, Nick would lose control of himself at the center and attack another child or a member of the staff. To stop the attack, I would hold Nick on the ground, my arms enfolding him—he was almost eleven, and only five inches shorter than me but heavier—and I felt we were in body-to-body knowing. I would have already endured his kicks and his spittle, but as we sat out on the grass, against the building, sometimes for an hour and a half, I was impressed, quite literally, by his body. And he was impressed by mine. I could feel him calming as I held him.

After his physical assaults, and then the holding, his manner of speech would change. When he was entering through the gate in the morning he would talk in staccato statements, and he would speak through anxious blinking eyes, or flittering hands, or a smile. His body expressed terrible anxiety. But after the holding p his voice seemed to emerge naturally out of body rhythm, as if he needed to find his voice from the body first.

When Nick came to EBAC he was classically autistic. It was only after several years that he started to speak. When I began to work with Nick, EBAC's clinical director, Frankie, told me that he was in his "symbiotic phase," by which she meant that although he was still psychically autistic he was "hatching"—a term that came from the great Hungarian psychiatrist Margaret Mahler. The clinical question was whether he would remain at that stage or whether he would make sufficient further progress to allow him to join an adolescent program. This would keep him out of Napa, the state mental institution, which by law had to take him if we did not succeed. Napa, we thought, meant a future of heavy vegetative medication: it was the end of a life. We knew of kids whom we lost to this tragedy, and when we did not succeed it was the realization of a terrible foreboding.

EBAC was on one of the approach flight paths to the Oakland Airport. We were nearly at the crest of the Berkeley Hills, and the planes would often pass perhaps five thousand feet above us as they descended toward the landing field some five miles away along the bay.

On occasion a plane's shadow would cast itself over the school's field. Some of the children would run for cover, others would freeze with alarm, and of course some seemed not to notice at all.

Nick was especially anxious about these overflights. He would rush to find me, hold on to me, and ask me what the planes were doing there. I would tell him they were on their way to the airport, and he said that this was very dangerous. Did I know how dangerous this was? I thought he meant that air flight was the problem, so I said I did not think it was so dangerous and asked him if he had ever been on a plane. He replied, "No, I am much too big. I could never get in one."

I then heard from his parents that they would face a problem each time they traveled south on the freeway, as this meant driving past the airport. As they came close to it, Nick would go into a violent panic, to the point where they had to hold him down, blindfold him, and put plugs in his ears until they were well clear of the area. No one seemed to know why he suffered so much agony about planes.

Then one day, with a tight smile on his face, he told me I was lying.

> "You're not telling me the truth, are you, Chris Ball?"
> "About what?"
> "You know what happens with airplanes but you are not telling me the truth."
> "What truth?"
> "They shrink to land."

I was stunned and at first I had no idea what he meant. He explained that the planes were big over the school but somewhere between the school and the airport there was a machine that shrunk them so they would land. I then learned over time that Nick was terrified that this machine would also shrink him and his family as they traveled toward the airport. He would never be able to get into a plane because at the airfield—which he could see from a distance—the planes looked "like small toys" and he would be too big to fit inside.

This was not a cognitive problem but a psychic one. He needed me to help him understand why he saw it this way, so we played with airplanes in our minds for some time until he eventually came to trust my version of reality. One day he told me very proudly that the family had driven past the airport and that he could now do this without panic.

Part One

18

Autistic and schizophrenic children live in a universe very different from our own. And nothing impressed this upon me more strongly than the times when we went on field trips. In the best of circumstances taking groups of children out of any school to visit the "outside world" is full of hazards. Will someone drift away and get lost? Will they fight? Will they abandon themselves to endless, raucous giggling, ignoring all attempts to keep them organized? But a field trip with the EBAC children was another experience entirely.

When newcomers to EBAC were recruited to go along on such expeditions, they had no idea what they were in for. So the first time I was told by the staff that we were going to the public swimming pool I was rather looking forward to the swim. Then the first child stepped down the stairs, put his foot in the water, and screamed bloody murder. "It's all right, Anthony," chimed Marie, a volunteer counselor, "nothing has happened to your body. See?" She reached down and touched his foot. "Go on, touch your foot, it's fine." Anthony, echoing the word "foot" as if it were now a mantra, repeatedly touched his foot, his laughter saturated with anxiety.

Much the same thing was happening with many of the other children. I did not understand at first why the children were screaming upon entering the water. I thought perhaps they felt it would dissolve them, but this was not the case. Their fear made a different kind of logic. If you look at your feet when you enter a pool you will see that the body is distorted below the water line. The children would see this and panic, assuming that the water was bending their bodies.

What they thought made sense in its own way, but of course it was not physically true. Our response was first to empathize with their anxiety and then to tell them that, however reasonable it seemed, it was not right. Yet our assurances would not have worked had they not been accompanied by empirical evidence. By repeatedly putting their bodies in and out of the water and repeatedly finding themselves still intact, the children began to trust their senses, our reasoning, and thus the evidence provided by reality.

What I came to realize was that almost all psychotic behavior was comprehensible if one could discover the underlying logic of thought.

And sometimes it was unintentionally and poignantly funny.

One day, as the parents were waiting outside the gate to take the children home, I noticed Larry rushing back into the lunchroom. He flew to the lunch box cupboard, opened the door, took out his lunch box, went to the lunch table, opened the box, closed it, went back to the cupboard, opened it, put the lunch box back inside, closed it, stepped back, then opened the cupboard, took out the box, and rushed out of the room. I chased after him and, on the trot, asked him why he had done this. "Because, I had to make up for lost time."

I was stunned.

In a way he was right.

He had brought his lunch box to school that day, forgetting that his class was going on a field trip where lunch was to be provided. From Larry's point of view he had therefore failed to have his lunch, in that he had not removed his lunch box from the cupboard, sat at the table to open it, and then taken it back to the cupboard. This moment in time had not occurred. So when he proceeded to do this at the end of the school day he was simply "making up for lost time."

On occasion the children would turn the tables on us, and their way of reasoning would trump the normals. This happened one day when we visited a church. After wandering around and exploring the pews and the sanctuary, we had an audience with the pastor. "What does God look like?" asked Nick. The pastor said that God did not have an appearance like the rest of us but was everywhere. Nick pressed on. "If he doesn't look like anything then why do you say he exists?" The pastor: "He exists in my mind through my faith in Him which is his way of allowing me to be in His presence." "So, if you *don't* have Him in your mind, then he doesn't exist?" asked Nick.

The pastor was now somewhat embarrassed and perplexed. Nick, meanwhile, was becoming decidedly uneasy. He, and probably some of the other children too, felt he was in the presence of an unfamiliar form of psychosis. The pastor could see that his failure to answer the question, and indeed some of the tenets of his own system of belief, were confounding Nick. The pastor was simply up against a nonbeliever. Like the other kids at EBAC, Nick desperately needed to believe that "we" (the adults in whom they placed so much trust) at least had some grounds for functioning in the way we did. Like Larry's lunch box routine, Nick's interrogation of the pastor was a rather brilliant challenge to ordinary ways of perceiving things.

That need to believe in our sanity was perhaps the most moving, and the most fragile, feature of working with psychotic children. They had never known what it was to be sane, but they could see that we lived our lives in a much less fearful universe than the one they inhabited. Of course they differed in their orientation to this juxtaposition, from envy and contempt to anxious adherence, but they generally hoped that proximal contiguity would magic them into a better world.

One thing they noticed was that, for the most part, we were able to transform our relation to reality in ways that reduced our risk of being crippled by circumstance. For example, if we got a flat tire on a field trip we would not react as though the tire was a damaged part of our body that required a visit to hospital for surgery. Our calm in the face of what felt to them like catastrophe, our ability to find a spare tire, jack up the car, replace the wheel and drive safely back to school, meant that we knew how to operate in the real, we could do things to the world that they could not imagine.

Up Against the Wall

Frequently during my two years at EBAC I saw that one or another of the kids would try to snatch a glimpse of, or try to hold on to, what there was about me that made it possible for me to live in the world. Larry would run by, pull on my shirt, hum, and run off. Tommy would shake his fists violently back and forth, hum very loudly and come up within a few inches of my face. He would stand very still and look deeply, it felt like, inside of me. Then he would back off, his fists going furiously, the humming returning. But as he ran off he always looked back, perhaps worried he had taken something from me and wondering if I was all right. Barry would come up behind me, hum, and pull my ear. Nick would steal a pen or a pencil and run off with it, yelling that he had my magic pen and now he would never give it back. An autistic child who never spoke would come up to me now and then, pull a few strands of hair from my head, and brush them across his lips before running away and casting them into the wind.

It is virtually impossible to honor the kinds of penetrating questions the EBAC children would pose. They often asked about what it was to be human, why we had to live in families, why we had to die. Like their attempts to hold on to something about me that could serve as proof of my ability to live in the world, these questions were attempts to get hold of some understanding of how I saw this world.

Ten months before I left EBAC we were all worried about Nick. The staff's understanding of his aggression was that, having come out of his autistic shell, having "hatched," he did not know how to relate to others. We understood his attacks on us and the other kids as attempts to form relationships. This made a lot of emotional sense to me, but of course as an explanation to the kids—and their parents—it didn't go down so well.

We had settled into something of a routine: I would persuade Nick to go with me to our space on the ground against the wall of the building, where I would hold him. He would then spit at me, or gouge my arms, or now and then kick my shins, but these were more like articulations in his body language of his many fears. Every day he would tell me who he was going to hit or kick or kill, and I would try differing ways to calm him down. It seemed that our physical contact, my holding of him, and time had the curative effect, and after half an hour or so we would trudge into the building and he would join his first class of the day.

One particularly soggy day, when sitting with him on the grass was becoming very uncomfortable, I asked him if he would accept our creating a story in place of sitting on the ground like this. We could sit on one of the benches in the playground.

"What story?" he asked.
"A story about an orange ship that travels around the world."
"Where is it going?"
"Well, right now I think it's in Alexandria."
"Who is on the ship?"
"Well, we'll have to decide."
"Who is the Captain?"
"Who do you think should be Captain?"
"Chris Ball, you are the Captain."

We agreed that the rest of the crew was made up of all the members of staff and all the children, and for the next six months we began each day with the story of the orange ship. Nick would now run through the gate yelling "The orange ship, the orange ship!" and off we would go to a bench that became the place of narrative. I was relieved that I no longer had to use all of my physical energy to hold this bulky kid, I did not have to suffer the discomfort of the damp grass, and most importantly Nick seemed to be helped by the form of a story.

Up Against the Wall

Each telling had the same structure. The ship would enter a port of call—Athens, for example—and I would tell a tale of how the various crew members visited the sites. We had a map, and I also introduced a bit of history, so we were also fulfilling a minimal educational dimension. After about ten minutes, Nick's hands would start to flap, he would blink, and I would know that he was on the point of breakdown. I would then stop and hand the telling over to him. For each positive venture I offered, he proposed a negative. If I said, "Larry climbed up to the Acropolis with Marie and Frankie and they looked at this ancient temple," Nick would say, "Larry and Marie and Frankie went up to the Acropolis, and Larry was eaten by an alligator and Marie fell to her death from the cliff and Frankie vanished into thin air." I would say, "Well, Nick, that's your version but I am sticking to mine."

For months there was no change to this structure, until one day Nick started laughing. He laughed and laughed. I had never heard him laugh like this before. Previously his laughter had been more like a form of screaming, but this was suddenly just ordinary. "You don't get it, do you, Chris Ball?" he chanted. "I don't get what, Nick?" "I am just kidding, just kidding!" For a moment, still I did not get it. But then I realized he was telling me that the horrifying tales of destruction, which I had been taking seriously, were now just jokes he was sharing. He was pulling my leg. We laughed together for the first time.

That was the end of the orange ship, but this experience with Nick taught me a crucial lesson. Although it was important, of course, to talk through a child's anxieties with them, it was also vital to keep the positive sides of life in mind. There had to be voices, outlets, for affection and safety, ways for the child to express pleasure in the course of an adventure (to make jokes), not just to focus on the fears that would lead to the self coming apart at the seams. Nick had made me captain of this ship and I was meant to offer a safe course through our travels, allowing him to express his anxieties but neither interpreting them nor ignoring them.

All of the therapists at EBAC found islands of health in their kids and would touch base with these, while also encountering their deep anxieties. Many of the staff members had been trained by Anna Freud in London. Their ethos was to identify and support those areas of strength in a distressed child so that ordinary means of self-protection could be utilized to support the child's capabilities. Nick was physically violent but also full of violent stories. By focusing on his narrative gifts, we were able to find room for violent thoughts so that they no longer needed to be acted out physically.

Anna Freud's psychology focused on the evolution of the self, from early infancy and toddlerhood, through the crises of family life, to latency, then to the resurrections of adolescence, the new formations of young adulthood and the subsequent psychological challenges posed throughout the life span.

In my view, movements through the stages of life, however enhancing and empowering, are also mini-breakdowns: with each newfound way of perceiving and communicating with the world, previously reliable assumptions are partly cast aside. Each step of the way involves loss and momentarily generates confusion.

In addition, it cannot be assumed that every crisis will be successfully negotiated. As D. W. Winnicott famously wrote, if our mothers (and fathers) are "good enough," then our breakdowns will be anticipated and parents will catch us before we fall into deep psychological repercussions.[2] They cannot spare us the pain of the breakdowns—this is inevitable—but they can be there to mitigate the full realization of these shocks. If parents can help us from breakdown to breakthrough, the positive side of new experience outweighs the negative. This then becomes a predominant logic of childhood.

Quite by chance I discovered, through the tale of the orange ship, that sharing a story could provide a narrative parallel to life at EBAC. By putting all of the staff and pupils on the ship, Nick found relief in the structured narrative reality. There were times when all of us at EBAC would break out into song—one song. Whether in the lunch-room, on a bus to a field trip, in the playing field, or wherever, the one tune we always belted out was "We all live in a Yellow Submarine." In those precious moments we were all "in this" together, and the gaiety of the Beatles, distilling the captive nature of human lives lived in the absurd, brought many of us on staff to tears.

When we cleared up after the children had departed the staff would assemble for a ninety-minute "debrief." During the day we would catch glimpses of complex or highly disturbed moments, and the afternoon group would be the time we gave ourselves to hear what had happened and to discuss issues that came up. In fact, we were all in a state of shock most days, and it took nearly two hours to recover from where we had been. Inside our own version of the yellow sub-marine, the world was taken as definitive. Once the day had ended we surfaced and realized where we had been. However individual this work was—and no therapist worked in the same way as any other therapist—we not only shared a common task but we also needed to be, to feel, part of a collective. Indeed, we needed to construct our own collective unconscious, to employ ourselves as a group mind, one capable of thinking through the shocking events of the day in the here and now of lived experience.

2

A Nation's Madness

ON THE OTHER SIDE OF THEIR reality, the children were increasingly bewildered over what seemed to be going wrong in the normal world.

The years 1967 to 1969 were harrowing, and seemed to be the culmination of a social psychosis that had been brewing since the assassination of JFK in November 1963. Murderousness appeared to have become an American way of life, not simply in the slaughter of the Vietnamese, but in the killing of seminal figures in the United States.

Malcolm X, an iconic leader for the African American community, was murdered in 1965. It was 1968, however, that seemed the apotheosis of madness. In April, Martin Luther King was assassinated, setting off riots in more than a hundred American cities. In June, Robert Kennedy was murdered. In just two months the two most important leaders in the country had been killed. The devastation wrought by these assassinations on the presumed sanity of American leadership was incalculable. One does not lose vital parts of the collective mind of a country without suffering, and in some respects the United States has never recovered from this loss of passionate but reasoned vision.

The trauma to America was portrayed in a garish nightmare in the summer of 1968 at the Democratic National Convention, where battles between the Chicago police and demonstrators outside the convention center soon spilled into the convention hall, as Mayor Richard J. Daley ordered so-called security officers to forcibly remove members of the media. This made CBS newscaster Dan Rather a national hero when he reported his eviction as it happened, and it gave birth to the clownishly left-wing Yippie movement, personified in Abbie Hoffman.

Typical of psychotic children, many of our students thought they had killed King and Kennedy. The day after each murder, some of them confessed to the crime, running around the playground as if being pursued, yelling "I did it. I killed him!" If something terrible had occurred in reality, it had to be their fault. It was impossible for them to believe otherwise. We, the normal people, could not possibly have done something like that. It must have been at their hands.

On such occasions the staff had a sort of drill. We would separate the kids from one another and hold them by their forearms, looking them directly in the eye and calmly telling them that no, they had not done it, and it was okay to be worried. Some would jump up and down or spit on the therapist, but firm physical holding and repetition of the statement that they were not murderers was sufficient over time to calm them down.

We may wonder, however, if the immediate and panicked response of our children spoke for the majority of Americans. Had we, indeed, murdered these leaders? How could we have stopped the murders from happening? JFK had gone to Dallas against the warnings of close advisers who informed him of the hate groups organized by the right wing. Martin Luther King had a premonition that he would be assassinated. Robert Kennedy, living in the aftermath of his brother's murder, took measures to protect himself—rushing through a hotel kitchen to his vehicle. But all of these premonitions and precautions failed to save their lives.

A year later the war in Vietnam came to Oakland and Berkeley when, in May, Ronald Reagan, then governor of California, ordered the National Guard to occupy Berkeley. Hundreds of people congregated at "People's Park." Many were shot and wounded, and one— James Rector—was killed. In his by then familiar hate-filled rhetoric, Reagan stated that there was no difference between the protesters and the Viet Cong. That link was enough to authorize the police and the National Guard to plunge into a psychotic confusion between an enemy abroad and their presumed doubles in America.

Each of these events in the real was deeply disturbing to the children, and after they were assured they were not responsible, weeks would be spent trying to answer the relentless questions: "Why was Martin Luther King killed?" "Why were there soldiers in Berkeley shooting people?" "Why was Robert Kennedy murdered?" When later that year oil wells off the coast of Santa Barbara emptied 200,000 gallons of oil into the Pacific, the television crews showed the devastation to sea life and coastal birds, and the children asked, "Why are we killing birds?"

Nick had an acute sensitivity to my own states of mind. He knew when I was in particularly good spirits or a bit subdued. "Chris Ball is not so happy today," he would say, scanning my face. I tried to answer him as honestly as possible, and sometimes I would share news from my life that seemed appropriate. "Well, our volleyball team lost in the final last night, so I am a bit bummed, Nick."

On the day that hundreds were wounded in People's Park I happened to be driving past it on my way home. I did not have a car radio and had no idea what was happening, but when I saw people running along College Avenue covered in blood I put several of them in my car and drove them to hospital. For the next three hours I continued to ferry the wounded, having to divert my path because the sheriff's officers were still shooting at anyone they thought might be part of a demonstration. The next day I joined the crowds at the park, and for some time after that I was absorbed in the politics of protest.

Nick knew where I lived. It is a feature of many autistic children that they have a need to "map out" the lives around them, locating people's position in space as well as remembering everything that has happened in the past. By knowing where people lived, how they got to work, and so forth, they could create a form of perception and memory that felt safe and reliable.

I knew that Nick would sense in me something of the events of those days, and he did. I told him that I had indeed seen some upsetting things, and when he wanted to know what they were I just repeated that they were upsetting. Any disturbing event in reality immediately called into question the children's own safety and the safety of those around them, and they relied on us to keep some form of hope alive; hope that we could keep the world sane so that their efforts to cross the boundary to sanity would one day be rewarded.

The mantra we had always used to reassure the children was "But you are safe; we are safe." In 1968, when we could no longer promise that the world was safe, we would say, "We are at the school and we are okay here." By the summer of 1969, however, the National Guard helicopters were flying over our school at low altitude to take demonstrators by surprise. On some days the children could look toward downtown Oakland and see smoke rising from the buildings. Our prior assurances that reality was comparatively safe now seemed absurd. What could we say? None of us looked forward to being at school on days when we knew we would be flooded with questions about the sanity of the world. We adopted a new phrase: "Try not to worry about it."

Until 1968 EBAC seemed to be a world apart from the wider social matrix of America. In contrast to the average normal American, these kids were unique because they were psychotic. But with the murders of King and Kennedy and wars in the streets of Berkeley and Oakland—between neighbors who were politically divided, even between members of families—the boundary between the children's psychosis and social madness blurred. Indeed, I was often struck by an irony: while the world surrounding us seemed in a constant state of flux and profoundly unpredictable, the children's psychoses were remarkably steady. Whatever their mental idioms were, they rarely changed, whereas in the world outside those delegated to report reality came up with radically different versions of it. In 1968, General William C. Westmoreland, in charge of the war in Vietnam, declared that we were winning; Walter Cronkite, the avuncular senior reporter for *CBS Evening News*, shocked the nation when he reported from a visit to Vietnam that America was losing.

In March 1968 members of the 11th Infantry Brigade of the U.S. Army massacred five hundred villagers at My Lai, an event that was made public in 1969. How was it possible that Americans—ordinary American soldiers, the heroes of the Second World War—could do something like *this?*

The sense that the country was gripped by some dark murderous force that was killing its leaders, and killing innocent people, seemed palpable. Was it accidental that the Pentecostal movement morphed into the charismatic movement, as clergy and flock displaced traditional Christian practices and sought leadership in a magical surrealist relation to their God? If the earthly leaders had been murdered, if the world had gone belly up, was it surprising that many people turned to some other world, to some other form of leadership, to provide them with a sense of safety and meaning? And if in so doing their movement could channel hate and madness into vilification of collectively designated enemies—be it the devil, his disciples on the left wing, or the Planned Parenthood movement—was that not in itself an organizing accomplishment?

It is easy enough to target such Americans as nuts. But the United States lost more than its innocence in the 1960s. Its moral deterioration constituted one of the most catastrophic collective mental breakdowns the world had ever witnessed.

Psychotherapists, especially those working with psychotic children, found themselves in an increasingly tenuous position. The majority of adults in America saw villagers in Vietnam as a direct threat to their safety and supported the war, but many of the veterans returned home transformed from their ordinary selves into psychotic individuals. War is never kind to the human mind. Many who fought in World War II or in Korea were driven mad by the boot camps that compelled them to abandon their humanity in order to kill and to survive. But Vietnam seemed different. These soldiers faced an enemy who did not fit the easy image of a bad guy; indeed, it was an open secret that those whom the Americans were ostensibly protecting in South Vietnam were friends by day and enemies by night. The war zone itself represented a massive denial of reality.

American historians, most notably Richard Hofstadter, had for decades talked about the "paranoid trend" in American politics.[1] Right from the beginning the Pilgrims had seen themselves as escaping the evils of Europe, destined to build a "city upon a hill" that would cast the beacon of righteousness across the seas, like the children of Israel, to fulfill a promise to their God. And even though these Puritans were "not quite right" in themselves—they were a fractured community,

Part One

32

denying serious psychological and criminal tendencies from the beginning—they were mad enough to establish a myth of innocence so powerful that it would intoxicate generations of Americans to follow.[2]

The Puritan delusion that America was an ideal land that could save those who emigrated was to become the core American legend. When the vast expanses of space and opportunity did indeed fulfill many dreams, this cemented the delusion that America was the promised land, provided by God for his chosen people.

Paranoia is really quite effective. It is defined by the paranoid's focus on monstrosity in the other. In Christianity this role has always been ably filled by the devil. For Americans it meant sustaining the notion that Europe was corrupt while they themselves were innocent. Following the American Civil War, which challenged the notion that viciousness was a property to be found only abroad, the United States was soon searching for external enemies so that it might once again restore its sense of purity.

The innocent self, or a nation convinced of its innocence, can maintain its stance only by projecting its destructive elements into a vilified opponent. The art of paranoia is to find a dustbin-other (person or country) sufficiently corrupt that it can become a convincing target for projection. The pleasure of evacuating the dark sides of humanity into the receptacle is profound.

America, like many a country, relies on finding an enemy it can hate. Through hate it projects its own violence, corruption, mindless ness, and greed into the other, which then contains America and ironically objectifies it. It is mirrored in its enemies—be they Russians, Vietnamese, Iranians, or anyone else. Because paranoia needs enemies it cannot breed affection and good relations to other countries except through bursts of self-idealizing action, such as pouring aid into countries where there are victims of natural disasters.

Although I do think normals differ in significant ways from schizophrenics, it would be untrue to say that non-psychotic people are without psychotic areas. Indeed, if we examine the American mentality we find that the core position sustaining the American way of viewing the world is paranoid and has been for centuries.

How might this background affect those who are pre-schizophrenic? Setting aside the issue of the individual etiology of schizophrenia, it is not difficult to see how the American need to polarize the world has led to a xenophobic attitude toward those who seem "different," "offbeat," or outside the American norm. During the 1960s the mantra from the right was "America: love it or leave it"—a phrase hardly lost on the kids of EBAC, who now and then would wonder how this applied to them.

If schizophrenics are already tragically different from the sane, their plight is made all the more difficult by the psychotic need of normals to sanitize their environment to avoid being contaminated by mental illness. The American Psychiatric Association's *Diagnostic and Statistical Manual of Mental Disorders*, which defines and categorizes and codifies all things in the study and treatment of mental disorders, is an American product that has created numerous new forms of mental illness. This says more about America's phobia regarding anyone outside the boundaries of what is considered normal than it does about what is actually wrong with people and why.

When the children of EBAC tried to find some way out of their psychosis, they faced a swirl of mad ideas generated by the world to which they were meant to adapt. Clinicians, trying to convince them that the ways of that world were safe and generative, struggled with the rhetoric of adaptation. In just ten years, from the mid-1950s to the mid-1960s, a country that had seemed to offer so much to so many— to the collective benefit of the white middle class, at least—had lost its allure.

Gifted with psychotic perceptions of reality, easily able to see through lies and deceptions, the children of EBAC were by now in deeper trouble. It seemed there was almost no good world left that they could aspire to join. Even though the staff continued to preach the value of participation in the American way of life, I doubt we were able to be convincing.

Indeed we found ourselves in an inverse relation to schizophrenia as we attempted to explain the way things happened in our world. Clinical work with psychotic children is a two-way street. Just as we might challenge and interpret their behaviors, they would do much the same with us. After being assured that they were not responsible for assassinations and wars, they would turn their schizophrenic astuteness to questions about the world. The psychotic child, who cannot take anything for granted, inevitably subjects our reality to a searching interrogation.

We were subjected to many interrogations from the children at EBAC, and we often found ourselves helpless to provide a rational answer for the madness of the so-called normal world beyond its walls. As our situations were inverted, a certain ironic relativism emerged in our work. Those who had been at EBAC for many years wore that ironic outlook very well. They knew we would be unable to provide lucid answers to such interrogations, and that our world's so-called sanity would often prove to be a house of cards.

What these experienced members of staff taught me was that the state of normality rests largely upon the capacity for denial. To live in our world we have to deny its reality. Joseph Sandler, one of my teachers at the Tavistock Clinic, believed that of all the needs we have in life, the foremost is the need for safety. D. W. Winnicott argued that all of us need to live, at times, within the realms of "illusion," and he focused his attention on the mother's provision of the illusion that the

A Nation's Madness

35

infant has created the world. Hunger produces a breast, or so it would seem, so for a period of time the infant experiences omnipotence, in the interests of the momentum of his true self and the establishment of his sense of inner personal reality.

The kids at EBAC, however, would see through the illusions that we live by. They would interrogate the clinicians about the illusions that comforted us and allowed us to live in a bearable world, and as we engaged in our in-depth conversation with them we would have to bear the erosion of the illusory in their own lives. To work with the psychotic person over a long period is distressing, not so much because of their psychosis, but because of how they deconstruct the defenses crucial to our own peace of mind. Some clinicians, understandably, elect not to inhabit that realm. Those of us who do are changed by these patients through their astute challenges to our own thoughtless assumptions and systems of safety.

It is important to make a distinction between "psychosis" and "madness." Schizophrenics are psychotic but they are not mad. Indeed, they are generally very frightened by madness and can often be phobic about coming into contact with it.

Madness refers to the creation of a chaotic state of affairs driven by the acting out of unconscious fantasies. A "mad scene," for example, is an episode that takes place in reality. It is considered abnormal, and it expresses the most primitive aspects of the human psyche— violence, sexuality, identifications, and paranoia.

Sophocles and Shakespeare wrote about madness, not about psychosis. They staged the madness endemic to all human families: a father's hatred of a son, a mother's jealousy of her husband, a child's rage against a sibling, a group's growing realization that it is following an illusion of coherence, defending against the reality of the incoherent. The family of origin is a launching pad for the parents and the children to engage in freelance enactments of shards of craziness—and no family escapes this madness.

Those who find themselves inside seriously mad families may sometimes opt for what we might think of as "the eccentric solution." An eccentric is a person who is odd or unusual, but who has found a way to control madness through forms of internal transformation of maddening scenes, often taming them through comedic representation. An eccentric will act outside the norms of behavior. This may cause distress to the normals, but it rarely violates their peace of mind because the eccentric has established a reliability in the performance of limited madness.

Schizophrenics seem to have sensed the danger of participation in family madness and to have developed curious and profound defensive structures against it. Often retreating into invented systems of meaning—outside the logic of family madness—they find ways to tiptoe through the fields of conflict. It is important to our understanding of the schizophrenic world that we differentiate it not just from the normal, but also from the mad, and the eccentric.

Our end-of-day staff meetings at EBAC were often curious occasions when we would spend half of our time recovering from encounters with psychotic children and significant time discussing the madness let loose through the actions of the American government, national and regional. Indeed, in the months before I left EBAC the meetings morphed into a small collective of clinicians who found respite from psychosis and madness by just talking it all through in our increasingly valued group process.

3

Frozen Psychosis

IN THE SUMMER OF 1969 I WAS on the move, headed to the University of Buffalo to earn a Ph.D. in English literature. Friends of mine from Berkeley were already there and had convinced me that it was an astonishingly creative department, where poets and novelists rubbed shoulders with French philosophers and traditional literary critics.

At first sight, Buffalo seemed like a very different America. It was a beautiful city full of majestic elm trees, Victorian wood frame homes, beautiful parks, the Niagara River and the Niagara Falls. It had been passed by in the mid–twentieth century when the St. Lawrence Seaway made it redundant. Like a vast exposition, it bore witness to the end of an American era, one that now seemed to have been its golden age. Some of the most elegant modernist buildings designed by Louis Sullivan and private homes by Frank Lloyd Wright dotted the city. The war in Vietnam, the travails of the civil rights movement, and all the anguish of contemporary America seemed beyond its imagination.

To settle in to the study of English literature was also to go back in time and mental space to a very different world. I was specializing in Jacobean drama, the American renaissance, and critical theory. For a number of reasons I found literary studies far more challenging than history, and I chose to go to Buffalo because I knew it would stretch me in ways that would shake me up, and this I needed.

Graduate students were required to teach composition to freshmen but they could also teach almost anything else they liked, and in 1970 I offered a course titled "Madness and Contemporary American Fiction." After I gave my opening lecture three or four students stayed behind. They were clearly in a very bad way. They had a hard time looking either at me or at one another, and one of them asked me how much I knew about schizophrenia, because he was a schizophrenic. I was shocked. I said I knew a bit about it, but was he sure this was the sort of course he should be taking? He said he didn't know what else to do. I asked whether he had been to the student health center and he said no, that he had seen the building but it looked weird, like a bunker, and he could not get himself to go inside. I said I would check it out for him.

I walked slowly across the campus. I was deeply moved by these kids, who of course reminded me of the younger ones I had worked with at EBAC, and, like a quiet drum, an idea kept crossing my mind: "You don't want to teach them—you want to work with them."

At the student health center it so happened that the director was free, and his secretary ushered me into his office. Lloyd Clarke, M.D., was a very calm, laid-back, turtleneck-wearing guy, with a slight goatee and smiling eyes. I told him about my class and then popped the question: "You know, I would rather work with these kids than teach them. Is there any chance I could get some kind of training here as a psychotherapist?" I told him about EBAC, my work in psychohistory as an undergraduate, and my own psychotherapy.

"Well," Clarke chuckled, reclining in his chair. "Now that would be a first, wouldn't it?" I said I guessed so. He looked up at the ceiling, smiling to himself, and was silent for about a minute, and then he said, "Well, I tell you what. I will have to run this by S. Mouchley Small (head of the department of psychiatry). What occurs to me is that, provided he agrees, you could work with one student and I would supervise you. And we would just see how it goes."

And that is how it went. After three months I was working two full days a week at the student health center, while also teaching courses and studying for my doctorate. Clarke was so pleased with how things were working out that he suggested we create a program for other people like me in the humanities who might like to work with students. Before long others were taking part, among them Robert Rogers, Murray Schwartz, and Norman Holland.

Clarke described himself as an "existential psychiatrist." He would listen without preconceptions to whatever was said to him, letting the patients teach him about who they were. He was convinced that if one listened like this, the person would eventually inform you of what he knew about his troubles and give you unconscious hints about how to approach helping him. Clarke would paraphrase what the person was saying and ask occasional questions, but he would never offer an interpretation, as he genuinely believed that he had no answer to what his patient was presenting. By working with Clarke and his staff I began to bring phenomenology and psychoanalysis together in the clinical setting, with a little help from my own therapy.

Clarke's advice to me was to have an important bearing on my work many years later with psychotic patients. Before one could begin to think through the unconscious fantasies and mad scenarios of psychotic personalities, it was crucial to absorb their view of reality. How did they perceive the world? Once this was grasped, the first step was to mirror this back to them so that, at the very least, they experienced someone understanding their world view.

Most of the people I saw at the health center were very disturbed, but Nigel was in a class of his own. A university department had referred him because of "violent vibes." Nigel—six feet five, with blond crewcut hair and startlingly blue eyes, and dressed all in black— arrived for his first session, sat back in his chair in the waiting room, and began cracking his knuckles. He did not check in at reception; he sat and stared straight ahead as if he owned the future. In a matter of seconds the other patients left the room and waited anxiously in the hall for their therapists. Eventually the secretary peered over the interior window and asked if she could help him. "I am here to see Mr. Bollas," he said, with his best android inflection.

Nigel did not look up when I entered the waiting room, and for a moment I was confused. Surely   please, God   this could not be my patient? I looked at the motionless figure in front of me and asked if he would be kind enough to follow me to my office. He stood up quickly and stiffly, as if called to attention, and I led the way.

First impressions can, of course, prove to be mistaken. But my first impression of Nigel was a lasting one. I was terrified.

He claimed to have no idea why he was in the room. He said he had been required to come, otherwise he would be removed from the university, which he said was unfair because he did not know the reason. He said he was a very moral person, and exact, and responsibly self-protective. He could not see why people had a problem with him.

I scheduled him for twice-weekly therapy. Every time he showed up, he emptied the waiting room.

Of course, I tried to talk with him about "violent vibes"—a highly unusual referral term that did seem quite apt. When I asked him why people might say this, he said he had no idea. He had never "behaved badly" in his entire life. Sure, he was into martial arts; smiling, he told me that when he walked along the pathways at the university he would look at oncoming people "to see how quickly and in what way I could kill them." He insisted this was purely a mental exercise, and he was very proud of it. I forced myself to say, "So, I suppose you have already figured out how you would kill me?" "Oh, sure," he replied, "that would be easy."

It is hard to convey how frightening this man was. I presented him to our weekly staff group on their insistence, because he had been so disturbing to everyone in the building. I knew very little about him, because he said next to nothing. I could report only that he was preoccupied with how noble and good he was and how the world should not put up with people who were evil or who did wrong. When I asked him how he thought this should be rectified, he replied that he was "a man of the law" and that if the laws were enforced then all the bad guys would get what was coming to them.

In some ways our sessions were rather routine. Nigel would describe his walk to the session, telling me about people he had seen along the way, describing how they looked and walked and how he would kill them. He spoke in a measured, hollow voice, with no affect at all, and was silent for long periods of time during which he would stare at me with his unreal wolflike blue eyes.

He described only one detail from his childhood. When he was a teenager he had a series of arguments with his mother; I said something about how awful this must have been, and his eyes welled up. It was the only sign of emotion I had seen from him in all our months of working together.

I had an idea that his sense of nobility and exactitude was based on a psychotic superego, and in one session when he told me again that he had imagined killing someone, I took the unusual step of asking him why he was working so hard on imagining things like that. "Do you ever give yourself a break?" I said. He looked bewildered.

Part One

42

A few sessions later he arrived upset for the first time. He had been to an ice cream parlor the night before with a woman he had invited out for a date. I was so shocked at the idea of this that it was hard for me to focus on what he said next, but he went on to tell me that when they entered they took a booth, then went to inspect the ice creams on display. When they returned to their booth it was occupied by a family of four: father, mother, and two boys. Nigel told them that they were in his booth and asked if they would be kind enough to leave. The father replied that he must be kidding, the place was empty and there were tons of booths. Couldn't they just go to the next one? Nigel insisted they move. He spoke in a way that must have been frightening, because his date ran out and disappeared. He remained standing alone at the table, persisting. Finally, the father, in fear for his family, bundled up his flock and they all left.

Nigel said, "Sometimes you just have to stand up against bullies like him."

"Well," I said, "you think of yourself as a hero, but actually you are a chicken shit."

I had no idea I was going to say this. In fact, as the words popped out of my mouth I nearly had a heart attack. Nigel flung a look at me that felt like it was the first of a series of murderous moves.

"You say you have to stand up against bullies, but look what you did. This great big part of your personality says to you that you *must* get that family out of there, and instead of telling this part of yourself to go fuck off and leave you and your date alone, what do you do? You cave in!"

When I said "you *must* get that family out of there" I altered my voice to imitate his metallic, android speech. I also stood up as I said this and pointed as if to a figure half my size, imitating a kind of giant.

Frozen Psychosis

I could never have foreseen what then took place. Heaving his chest as if he were engaged in an aerobic prequel to murder, Nigel let out a bizarre sound, audible all the way out to the waiting room. The secretary said later that she had never heard a sound like this, and neither had I. It took thirty or forty seconds to complete itself, from the first "AAAAAAHHHHHHHHHH" to "GGGGGGGGGUUUUUU-UUUHHHHH," followed by a complete stoppage as if he could not breathe, to the conclusion when he doubled over in convulsive laughter. He could not stop laughing for about ten minutes. I have never seen stranger behavior in my entire life.

"Say that again," he said.

"Again?"

"Yeah, exactly as you did. And stand up like you did."

So, I repeated the same phrase and in the same way, and once again Nigel rolled over with laughter.

From that moment on when he entered the waiting room he would say to the secretary, "Tell Mr. Bollas that the Chicken Shit is here." In the sessions, he would frequently refer to himself like this, and he used the phrase in countless different ways as he absorbed the idea that he had not been able to get out from under the strength of his sense of obligation, and he linked his need for overwhelming power to his domination by a brutal mother and siblings. This breakthrough, such as it was, was occasioned by his ability to laugh at a part of himself that until then had ruled his life.

Although Nigel was certainly a deeply disturbing presence, he was not actively psychotic. He suffered what we might think of as a *frozen psychosis*. People such as him exhibit few if any evident signs of psychotic thinking; this part of them has been encapsulated in a frozen, split-off state that allows the self to appear more or less normal. Their dilemma may therefore elude recognition, whereas in schizophrenics or manic-depressives the psychosis is obvious and is therefore more likely to be treated.

The French writers André Green and Jean-Luc Donnet might describe Nigel as suffering from a blank psychosis.[1] Instead of producing ideation, the mind rids itself of all but a few select thoughts. It also produces negative hallucination—rather than hallucinating nonexistent objects, it negates the presence of objects that are present in the world around them. Nigel's imaginary killing of people he encountered was akin to a mental martial art in which he eliminated his others. One striking feature of this pattern was that if he met someone he had previously "murdered," he acted as if the person no longer existed.

Often hysterics gather in groups that cultivate a psychotic state of mind. I was referred another Buffalo student, a young woman with blond hair streaked with black lowlights, black nail polish, dressed entirely in black, who said she was a witch and was part of a coven. Jonelle would anxiously tell me about herself, and I said very little. We met twice a week for just over a year. She was worried about the coven, afraid that some of their "visions" were bordering on "the insane." The group had developed a private language with encoded physical gestures and invented an imaginary world in which friends and staff would be given fictive names.

Jonelle felt she could no longer control the boundary between that world and the real world. She started calling classmates and teachers by their fictive names, in violation of the coven's agreement that their private reality must never be revealed to the real world it replaced. She was now sure that one of her fellow witches intended to murder her and had sought protection. When I asked what sort of protection that was, she reached for her purse and pulled out a small toy pistol.

Frozen Psychosis

At no point did she lament her participation in the coven's world. She had, however, become alarmed by an increasingly powerful voice in her head that was telling her to kill one of her fellow witches if she was "not to be among the damned." I asked her if she would please give me the toy pistol, which I said would more likely get her into harm rather than protect her.

I told her that she was not in danger of any actual physical harm from her fellow witch, but that she had departed from the real world for such a long time that she had now reached a point where she was hallucinating and actually losing contact with it. She stared at me. The session was running over time, but I did not have another patient so we stayed in the room together for about two hours.

Eventually she said, "Do you think I could just go home?" She meant, could she leave the university and return to her family in St. Louis. I asked what home was like, and she said both her parents were kind people. I said if she allowed me to make a referral for her to see a therapist in St. Louis, I would agree to this and help her by facilitating a temporary leave of absence from the university. I asked what she would do in St. Louis. She said that family meals felt like healing moments, and she loved hearing what her parents did at work. Her mother worked in the garment district, her father for the fire department, and they were full of stories that amused and intrigued her. And during the day? She said she would return to reading and writing poetry. She asked about the other witches in the coven. What could she do to protect herself from them? I said there was good and bad news. The bad news was that very likely they would shun her and never speak to her again, but this was also the good news. She smiled briefly and said that was actually a part of the pact, and I helped her make arrangements to go home.

Some months later I received a note from Jonelle. She let me know that she was still hearing voices, and she wrote, "the world sometimes goes vivid on me," from which I guessed she was experiencing visual hallucinations. But she said she was deeply grateful to be able to speak English again and to take part in the world.

Clarke had taught me a vital lesson: try to find out what the person knows about how to help themselves, help them learn from their own self-therapy techniques, and then work with this. Nigel had identified with a powerful ideal self, which saved him from committing violent acts of harm. If he could develop a sense of humor, he might get out from under psychotic sanctimoniousness and find some thread of help that, with luck, might see him through the really rough times. Jonelle knew that if she returned home to be with her parents, just hearing tales from ordinary life, she could move back from a slide into psychosis.

Some years later, Masud Khan would term this "self cure," but he regarded it as part of the self's psychopathology. Both he and Winnicott considered it virtually a moral imperative to break this down, as it could only be a part of the false self's organization. At times this may be true, but they failed to grasp something appreciated by Clarke and others: that such devices are often attempts to recuperate from trauma, and as such can be of immense value during the course of a life.

Nigel kept his fearsome image going for a long time—only slightly modified by our work—but I think he had privately begun to foster a more relaxed and forgiving internal world. When she returned to St. Louis, Jonelle used her false self to help her start to negotiate with reality. One has to understand how the much-maligned false self can serve as a vital transitional personality that protects a person while he or she is undergoing inner change, something that can be deeply reassuring to people who have been privately mad.

4

Free Speech

ALMOST WITHOUT EXCEPTION, the undergraduate students I taught were terrified of English composition. Their essays were often sad, restricted forms of reporting on a poem or a short story. They had few ideas of their own.

One day I said to a freshman composition class, "Tell you what. I am going to read a poem and then I'm going to write on the blackboard whatever comes to your mind. Just give me images, words . . . I don't care. But don't *think*."

I read the poem (it was by Sylvia Plath) and very soon they were peppering me with words and images—from Buffalo, other parts of the country, landscapes, people. In five minutes the large blackboard was full of "ideas." We read it together and then I asked them to connect the images with chalk lines. Two or three of the students got up and began to join one image to the next, until we had a web of connections crossing the board.

We mulled over our collective response and discovered some aspects that seemed to stand out—the basis for a potential essay. I then assigned them another poem to read that night and told them to do alone what they had seen on the board. I urged them not to think, just to write what came to mind. In the next class I had each of them pass their associations to another student and asked them to connect images with lines. I collected a few responses at random and read them out to the class, then asked if anyone could see what this writer might be saying about the poem.

At first they were shy. It was not difficult to see from their associations where they were headed, but they needed reassurance in order to have faith in what their unconscious had produced. Over the next weeks I had them repeat the exercise several times, then I met with each student individually for a discussion, and from there they went off to write essays.

Looking back, I can say this was perhaps my first deliberate use of free association as an educational method. This would be an important step in the development of my belief that, if one can gain access to people's free associations, if they can just speak from deep within the self, they will tell us a great deal about their core created truths.

How did I know that calling Nigel a chicken shit would prove transformative? I didn't. But by then I had become sufficiently trusting of my unconscious associations to permit myself, at times, simply to say what crossed my mind. Provided such comments are offered for what they are—associations and not cultivated truths—there is a remarkable freedom and potential in the associative process itself.

Many psychotic patients will refuse to discuss their hallucinations or report exactly what the voices have said to them. But if helped to associate—or "free talk," as I like to call it—then they, like anyone else, will begin to reveal the threads of thought that are preoccupying them.[1] A simple question such as "So tell me, what did you do yesterday?" might be expected to elicit only a report about events in reality, but as psychotic people begin to describe ordinary movement in the quotidian they will reveal, in the leaps from one topic to another, chains of ideas inherent in the unconscious.

In addition, talking about everyday reality instead of struggling with their internal disturbance feels anchoring and safe. When they realize, in time, that they are nevertheless disclosing their thoughts, they may have an initial paranoid reaction, but generally they then discover that this is a mental process that is not harming them; indeed, it is generative and can be nourishing.

In the second half of the twentieth century it was practically a given in psychiatry that one never asked about the free associations of a schizophrenic or manic-depressive patient. It was argued that such approaches would only deepen their illness by sending them into the chaotic realms of the primary process. Instead, one should keep them firmly rooted in reality, shoring up defenses, and deliberately not taking up any unconscious meaning resident in what they might be saying. The manic-depressive's thought processes were dismissed as "loose associations" that lacked coherent thought. The schizophrenic's associations were seen as meaningless "word salads" with no inherent logic. Indeed, many people trained in psychiatry and psychology were averse to talking at all with their psychotic patients. They would greet their attempts at communication with a smile and a sort of condescending, avuncular tolerance. The idea was to wait it out and then bring the patient "down to earth," often upping the medications or extending the stay in hospital.

My experience had taught me to think very differently. I knew there were people such as Harold Searles, Bryce Boyer, and Peter Giovacchini in the United States, and Wilfred Bion, Herbert Rosenfeld, and Hanna Segal in Great Britain, who believed in listening to the free associations and unconscious communications of the schizophrenic person. Given what I learned from my work with Nick at

EBAC, I felt that if a psychotic child could teach me how to help him by enthusiastically embracing a story, then we should be giving the psychotic adult a similar opportunity. From Nigel I learned that I could trust the freedom of unconscious association to unlock the seemingly incarcerated self. From my "normal" students, almost psychotically paralyzed by having to think about a poem, I learned that simply asking them for associations produced a highly creative unconscious reading.

It is important to my argument in the chapters to follow that we dwell a bit longer on the therapeutic role of free association, in both analyst and patient, and on how it can be used to work with schizophrenia and other forms of psychosis.

For five years during the 1980s I conducted a workshop in New York on "Unconscious Communication." The clinicians in the group were highly experienced practitioners from diverse backgrounds. We would meet for three hours at a time and listen to a case. But this would be an unusual type of clinical presentation. The presenter was asked to eliminate all of his or her own comments and associations. No background information of any kind was to be provided; no history, no explanations of names mentioned, not even the patient's gender or age. All we would hear would be the stream of ideas, in the patient's words.

Every few minutes I would stop the presenter and ask the group to associate. Interpretations were forbidden. Instead people were encouraged to offer associations from life, or feelings, or images, or to dwell on what might be evoked by individual words that struck them. We were not to ask the presenter questions of any kind, and when voicing our associations we were to avoid looking at the presenter so that we would not be influenced by any facial expressions. While we were speaking, the presenter would take notes that would later help us understand in what ways we were making contact with the patient's unconscious.

It would take about two hours to go through two consecutive sessions presented in this manner. Then we had the task of summing up what we *thought* we had thought. Inevitably the group, which had become a sort of collective unconscious mind, would have formed various Gestalts. Then the presenter had half an hour to tell us about how what we had thought linked up to the case.

I very much regret that we did not transcribe these meetings. They demonstrated how, with no contextual information but simply on the basis of seminal signifiers, or protean images, or character features that presented themselves to the group, we were able to grasp aspects of this person through our own unconscious attunement.

I conducted similar groups in other cities on differing continents. Although the clinicians varied in their abilities—a lot depended on how effectively a group could form a collectively receptive unconscious mind—the participants were always quite astonished to discover how accurately we could read many aspects of the patient in this way.

The core axiom of this approach was that a group of people developed an unconscious collective mind, which if listened to by the analyst in a state of reverie, would communicate unconscious ideas and emotions that could be identified.

We all live in groups, and the vital groupings of our lives—as small as a family or as large as a nation—all develop their own "collective unconscious." Jung's famous phrase refers to how each culture inherits and passes along its own particular social unconscious. Group therapists trained in the models proposed by Bion and A. K. Rice discover how a group of strangers will quickly divide certain functions among them in order to develop the mind of that particular group.

The raw experiences of life—love, hate, envy, anxiety, hope, despair, bewilderment, madness—enter the group as powerful emotional states, and the ability to process these will depend on the members of the group forming a collective mind. One person might be nominated as the group's "feeler" who senses out emergent emotions, undergoing what seems to be a private affective experience that proves, in fact, to be a part of the entire group's latent and emerging experience. Another member may be the group's "organizer-speaker," who puts the feeler's emotions into phrases and units of thought that help the group transform uncomfortable states into something more reflective.

This approach allows one to see how a group will form its own mind, then lose it, and then find it again through a collective process. Working with therapists to develop a group mind capable of processing the raw materials of a session was a way of exercising unconscious thinking, but it was also a means of developing and testing the capacity of individuals to form a group that could become its own entity, with different functions delegated to different members.

At EBAC when we met every afternoon to report on the day, we were returning to our collective unconscious. This was a way for our group to gather its wits, to shift and change functions within the collective, and to prepare for the next day. Weekly staff meetings at the university health center at the University of Buffalo were also a return to this collective, the formation of a group mind. A matrix developed over time, composed of many differing clinicians with widely divergent perspectives, who nonetheless quite unconsciously (and naturally) composed this separate sense: the creative process of a group of colleagues thinking together. The work groups on free association depended entirely on the creation of a group mind in which roles and functions were unconsciously allocated among members who, as they thought out loud, contributed to the perceptual acuity and intuitive

Free Speech

53

comprehension of the unconscious lines of thought reported by the individual clinician.

What does this have to do with working with schizophrenics? Quite simply, they are not able to take part in any collective unconscious process. Their break from what we term reality is so severe that they lose touch with the national unconscious, the regional or local unconscious, their family—indeed, with everyone. Hopefully, if those who work with them have some knowledge of group process and of their own role within a collective mind, and if they can function as a holding environment for the materials projected by the patients, then they will be able to help them find ways to make, and maintain, contact with others.

5

A Magical Bench

IN THE SUMMER OF 1973 I moved to England to train as a psycho-analyst. The Institute of Psychoanalysis in London is the training body of the British Psychoanalytical Society. Candidates spent their first year in analysis and did not attend seminars until the following year. They usually began their first training case in April of their second year, and their second by the following autumn. Most qualified in four years and were elected into the British Psychoanalytical Society. About a third of those doing the training were from abroad, especially from Europe and South America, and about half of these returned home after they qualified.

Unlike any other psychoanalytical training institute at that time, the British Society welcomed lay candidates. The institute had taken to heart Freud's advocacy of lay analysis, and trainees came from many spheres of life, including philosophy, literature, physics, fine art, anthropology, business, even sport. This commitment to lay analysis had been present since the beginnings of the society, when Adrian Stephen (the brother of Virginia Woolf), James and Alix Strachey, and others infused the training with the ethos of the Bloomsbury Group. Of course there were also plenty of medical doctors and psychiatrists among the candidates (notably D. W. Winnicott, arguably the world's leading pediatrician of his time), but they did not regard their medical training as the basis of their psychoanalytical thinking. What they learned about analysis, they would insist, came from the couch. They learned from experience.

One would have thought that with the presence of so many members of the intelligentsia, the institute would have been a rather heady place. But it wasn't.

First there was a curious edict: during our training we were instructed *not* to read widely in psychoanalysis. In fact we were only to read those essays assigned for our seminars, and during our first year of psychoanalysis we were told not to read any psychoanalysis at all. Reading was thought to interfere with the pure experience of being in analysis. We had to know it first and foremost from within. This was very much in the spirit of British empirical philosophy. The evidence of our analysis had to be built up through the siftings of each session, week after week, month after month. We were scientists, of sorts, and the society's meetings were called "Scientific Meetings."

Second, the British had an antipathy toward theory not backed by "empirical" evidence. During the training, theory was invariably introduced through the medium of long case histories. These cases were not summaries of treatments but, as far as was possible, highly detailed verbatim accounts of exactly what the patient and the analyst had said. Any commentary had to wait for the discussion, and people were therefore free to come to their own view of what they thought was really taking place in the session.

There is a lot written these days about so-called "evidence-based" therapies. I know of no better evidence of how clinicians practice, why they do what they do, and how it works than a meticulous presentation of what is said in sessions between patient and analyst. The massive

Part One

body of analytic work from over a century adds up to a comprehensive catalogue of evidence-based presentations for all to consider.

Stuart Schneiderman, a professor of English whom I got to know at Buffalo, went on to have an analysis in Paris with Jacques Lacan. We occasionally shared notes about our separate experiences of training in England or France and it was clear that, unsurprisingly perhaps, the French took a very different approach to training from the British. French psychoanalysis was still embroiled in the passionate throes of 1968, and candidates there were avid readers of philosophical authors, especially Claude Lévi-Strauss, Louis Althusser, Baruch Spinoza, G. W. F. Hegel, and Martin Heidegger. For them, psychoanalysis was, above all, an important movement in Western thinking. Freud was read like the Talmud. Theory was everything. Psychoanalysis, which anyway existed in the realm of abstraction, had to be considered primarily from an intellectual point of view.

My own thinking, however, had evolved out of my various practical clinical experiences in America. When I arrived in London to begin my training, the first thing I did was to take up a post at the Personal Consultation Centre (PCC), a mental health clinic across the street from King's Cross Station.

Newly arrived in the country, I turned up there on my first day to find myself confronted with a bit of culture shock. After winding my way up the stairs I arrived on the dot, but no one was to be found. The door was open, so I sat in the waiting room and waited. After about fifteen minutes a young woman appeared. She said, "Oh, hello . . ." and she stopped because she did not know who I was. I could, heaven forbid, be a patient. "Hello. I am Christopher Bollas." "Oh dear, of course, how nice to meet you," she said. "I won't be a minute," and she disappeared through one of the doors, shutting it behind her. A moment later Myra Chave-Jones arrived. She had visited me in

Boston to interview me for my job at the PCC, and when she saw me she stepped back, put her hand over her mouth and raised her eyebrows, and I thought she might be in shock.

"Ah, so . . . there you are."

"Yes, hello."

"Tea?"

"I beg your pardon?"

"Would you like some tea?"

"No thanks, I've had breakfast and . . ."

"Good . . . I'll be back in a minute."

And she too disappeared behind her door.

It seemed as though I waited forever, but suddenly, almost at the same time, both my new colleagues emerged from their respective doors and were ready to receive me. This was the most downbeat reception I had ever received in my life. Not a word about how I was, what was the trip like, was I settled in—none of that. Later I came to understand that to have asked such questions (at least in those days) would have been considered quite inappropriate. They would no more impose such a question upon someone than they would want it asked of themselves, so silence was a kind of quid-pro-quo.

It took many weeks to settle in and become acquainted with this very different style of communicating. But it was exciting to be there, and the government under Edward Heath created quite a Dickensian mood by turning most of the streetlights off at night to save energy.

One morning during my second week of work I heard a loud explosion from the direction of King's Cross Station. It was a dull, heavy, thudding sound, and I imagined that a train must have run through the barrier at speed. Soon hundreds of people emerged from the underground station, bloodied and covered in soot, clutching broken cases and umbrellas. It turned out to have been one of the many bomb explosions set off in the 1970s by the Irish Republican Army. But, in very much the same spirit of detached calm that had greeted my arrival at the PCC, my colleagues just got on with their work as if nothing of real significance had just happened. I realized that I was seeing at first hand something of that legendary wartime spirit I had read about. The British were unflappable.

Most referrals to the Personal Consultation Centre came from University College Hospital, the University of London, the Marie Stopes Clinic, the Tavistock Clinic, or local physicians. Although we did good work, there were days when we would have only five or six patients visiting, so we had more than enough time on our hands. I was pleased with this arrangement, as it meant I could get on with trying to finish my Ph.D. (on Melville), but now and then we had the occasional drop-in patient.

The English were not really the drop-by sort of people, and it was always rather a surprise when anyone came in unannounced. One day I found a roughly dressed but imposing man in his fifties standing in the waiting room.

"Can I help you?"
"You American?"
"Yes."
"It says Personal Consultation."
"Yes . . ."
"I would like one."
"You would like a personal consultation?"
"Yeah, that's right, a personal consultation."
"Well, that's fine. How about you step into my office?"
"Okay, guv'nor."

A Magical Bench

For about an hour this man talked about how he was having a bit of a rough time and did not know what to do with himself. He didn't like the general practitioner he was meant to see and anyway didn't believe in that sort of stuff. He assured me he was not looking for money or handouts or anything like that—he knew how to get assistance.

"It's me head."

"Your head?"

"Yeah, that's right. Something's gone wrong."

"What does it feel like?"

"I'm lost. Don't know where I am."

"How long have you felt this way?"

"Well . . . don't know . . . but it's recent."

"Do you have headaches, problems with your vision or walking?"

"No, no, none of that sort of thing. It's more a sort of personal thing."

"You feel different."

"Yeah that's right, guv. I feel like I've lost me bearings."

"Have you ever had this kind of feeling before?"

"Yeah . . . yeah, I have."

"Really?"

"Yeah."

"So, what did you do before when you felt this way?"

"Well, I went to some hospital, you know, down the road, but they couldn't find anything. And me G.P. says it's me drinking, but I don't drink much. I like the outdoor life and they say I should spend more time inside, but that's not me, is it?"

"It's not you?"

"No, none of that is me."

"So what did you do to help yourself when you felt this way?"

He leaned back in his chair, his expression changed, and he gave me a huge smile of relief.

"I go to me bench, I do."
"Your bench?"
"Yeah, I call it me magical bench."
"Really?"
"Me magical bench."
"So, where is it?"
"It's . . . you know . . . over there in Gordon Square, almost hidden in the bushes."
"So it's not far."
"No, it's really close by."
"Well, here's what I think. I think you should go to your bench and just sit on it for as long as you like. See if it helps you this time. We close at five p.m. I am here every day, so if your wonderful bench doesn't help you this time, come back and see me and we'll sort something out."
"Oh, Doc, you're a clever one, aren't you."
"Sorry?"
"You knew this all along. You knew how to help me."
"Well, you helped *me* actually."

He was standing up, collecting his things.

"Well, I think I'll be going. I know I'll feel better—and I don't want anyone else sitting on me bench, do I?"
"And you will be back, for sure, if it doesn't work for you this time?"
"Oh, Doc, it will work. It always does."

A Magical Bench

61

I never saw this man again, and I wondered whether I had done the right thing. Should I have insisted he go to hospital for a checkup? What if there was an underlying organic condition causing his problems? But he had been very clear. Odd and unkempt as he was, intimidating and out of place as he appeared, he knew he was in emotional trouble and he knew what to do to help himself.

In 1975 I moved on to the Tavistock Clinic, where I was to train in the newly formed adult psychotherapy program. The plan was for candidates to study for four years and learn how to do individual psychotherapy (long-term and focal), couples therapy, group psychoanalysis, and forms of community work, such as secondment (assignment) to a G.P.'s surgery (office). The Tavi, as it is commonly known, was by then an internationally recognized center, known for its leadership in the world of the psychotherapies. Almost all schools of thought—psychoanalytic, systems theory, field theory, gestalt theory, focal theory, encounter theory, and more—existed in the building in one form or another. The Tavistock Institute of Human Relations was an offshoot of the clinic devoted to the study of group behavior, providing highly sophisticated forms of consulting for organizations.

One of the reasons the Tavi was world renowned was the fact that Wilfred Bion had worked there during his early years as a psychoanalyst. The Tavi approach to object relations owed an enormous amount to his theory that any mind was, in itself, a group process governed by assumptions that were often driven by anxiety, hate, envy, and greed or by those defenses people set up to rid the self of contact with those elements, such as idealization, hope, euphorias, and so forth. The mind was a constant movement of elements often unlinked to one another and thus outside the realms of consciousness. For Bion, any group of people would, in effect, mirror this internal organization and would be governed by many of the same conflicts taking place in the individual.

Bion was intrigued by the ordinary psychotic parts of all people and, in particular, by schizophrenia. Those of us supervised by his former analysands (such as Robert Gosling, then director of the Tavi) or his students were inevitably trained in the Bionian vision of self and group. Although he was nominally a Kleinian, Bion's psychology was a new way to view the self and its relation to the other. It was, and still sustains, a profound rethinking of human psychology.

None of my patients at the Tavistock were schizophrenic, but I had schizophrenics in my private practice, which I had started while working at the Tavi. It was inevitable that Bion's vision would influence my way of thinking. Indeed, I learned much about the psychotic nature of selves from conducting a Tavi group, a process derived from Bion's methodology. The group analyst remains silent for most of the ninety-minute period. In doing so, the group is left to itself: to talk, to think about the analyst and individual members, and most of all to experience what begins to happen to the group as an entity over this span of time. As leadership shifts between the members, as the themes fragment for numerous reasons, a Tavi group is not long delayed in reaching deep forms of anxiety and hate, envy and insatiable greed, manic hope and idealization. These mutating forms crystallize issues endemic not only to the human species but also to the individual ailments of each and every member present.

When the group psychoanalyst makes an interpretation it is addressed only to the group, never to an individual, and it is directed at the primitive state of the group's mind. So, for instance, if the group had concentrated on and was being critical of a member whom it felt was taking up too much of the group's time, the analyst might say something like "the group thinks it has talked too much but now does not know what to do about talking." It is clear that this approach shifts the emphasis from the act of a person who is talking too much to the idea of the person as doing something that is a vital part of the group itself. The over-talking person is not to be separated from the group; indeed, another comment by the psychoanalyst, further along, might be "the group is unsure whether to kill talking or not."

Usually one or two people would drop out after a few weeks, and it would not be long before those who remained felt relief that no single one of them was going to become an isolate, successfully scapegoated by the group. On the other hand, neither was the group going to find some way to get the psychoanalyst to rescue them through personal interventions of a predictable type that made him or her a sort of friendly and reliable human presence.

The analyst seemed to come from a different world. We might say he functioned from within the mind itself, a sort of verbal interlocutor between unconscious elements and between the unconscious and consciousness.

To this might be added that the Bionian psychoanalyst almost emulated the very psychotic process that he addressed. To undergo training in this form of group psychoanalysis, much less conducting such a group over some years, would at times be harrowing. It was, however, exceptionally apt education in the art of being with the schizophrenic, much like learning Latin is essential to grasping the heart of classical and medieval texts. My Tavi training helped me to *see* the interplay between psychotic elements within the individuals I met with in my private consulting room. However simplistic it sounds, the fact that I had witnessed that interplay in the theater of the group—in which individuals literally enacted one role or another from the theater of the mind—made it far easier to see those parts expressed by individuals: either in what they talked about, how they talked about it, how they behaved as they talked, or how they related to me as they spoke.

6

Listening to a Different Logic

IN 1977 I BEGAN WORKING AS A psychoanalyst in full-time private practice. I saw my patients at my home, a large Edwardian house in North London. The pathway to my consulting room was along the side of the building, and patients passed through an external doorway into an enclosed courtyard and entered through a rear door. The waiting room was large and comfortable, with bookshelves and pieces of pottery.

Like most European analysts, I sat directly behind the patient, who reclined on a couch—in this case an ordinary single bed covered with a woolen throw. All I could see of my patients in this position was the top of their heads and their feet. Otherwise my gaze was directed into middle space as I listened. Or perhaps I should say "as I took them in," because listening is only part of the work of the psychoanalyst. The room was enclosed by thick brick walls so that it was almost soundproof. No noise from inside the house was audible, but through the window one could hear birdsong, the sound of children's voices as they ran to and from school. The view from a large window was of a plane tree twenty feet from the room and, beyond, the pale blue skies of London.

I lived in this room five days a week, ten hours a day, for almost twenty years.[1]

Every patient is different, a unique force of personality. I can recall the *psychic textures* of each and every one of them in the same way one can evoke the internal impressions of Mozart or Schubert. A few were psychoneurotic but most were severely disturbed. During this period I analyzed psychotic people—not people with psychotic parts of the self but those who were either manic-depressive, schizophrenic, paranoid, or suffering from a hysterical psychosis.

Each of these remarkable people presented me with serious challenges, but in some ways no differently from my psychoneurotic patients, and in many senses they were more accessible than those who were less primitively disturbed. What struck me about my schizophrenic patients was that, if they were speaking and if they had reached a point of trusting me, they could become remarkably frank about what they thought. In other words, given time and the intensive listening of a clinician, they could change.

It is true that many schizophrenics who have been heavily medicated, hospitalized for a long period of time, and left with no one to talk to can revert to forms of thinking, speaking, and behaving that do fit the common stereotype of a person who cannot mentalize or use the symbolic order. But we need to separate out the causes of such deterioration. Are they intrinsic to and characteristic of schizophrenia, or are they, sadly, more often true of the schizophrenic who is *abandoned*—left in a degrading state that results in psychic retreats that compromise mental function?

Megan was twenty-seven when she began analysis with me. Nearly six feet tall with cropped red hair, Megan was an extraordinarily imposing person. Diagnosed as schizophrenic when she was seventeen, she had been in mental hospitals twice, once for six months. She had been heavily medicated until her mid-twenties and then, supported by her G.P., she made the decision to stop this course of treatment.

When she arrived for her first session, on a Monday, Megan remained seated in the waiting room when I entered and showed no sign of having registered my presence. I stood in silence for about a minute and then said perhaps she would prefer it if we talked first in the waiting room before going into the consulting room. "Yes, thank you," she said. She was wearing wooden clogs and carefully slid her yellow stocking feet from the shoes and gently slid them to her left. She spent much of the hour gazing at her clogs.

We sat in silence for the remainder of the hour, and when the session ended I told her the times when I could see her. We determined that she would come five days a week, beginning the next day.

On Tuesday she entered the consulting room, walked to the couch and sat up on it looking out the window. She slid her feet from her clogs—orange socks this time—and remained motionless.

I sat in my chair. We said nothing. The hour ended and I said it was time to stop. I got up and, as was my custom, I opened the side door, stepped out into the passageway, opened the external door and stood waiting for her to leave. As she went past me she said, "Thank you."

For the next weeks Megan said very little. Then she began to speak, but in a curious way.

"Think . . . [pause of twenty seconds] . . . they saw it but, well . . . [pause of two minutes] . . . Louise wouldn't go there . . . [pause of five minutes] . . . nothing really . . ."

I had no idea who Louise was, or what was meant by the "it" that they saw, or indeed who "they" were.

This is how Megan spoke for the first year or so of our work.

Sometimes she would cry—I would see her taking her hands to her cheeks and wiping them—but it would be inaudible.

It took a long time for me to adapt to her logical structures or, to put it differently, to learn how to think in her idiom. She reminded me of a former patient who did something similar—speaking disjointedly, with frequent long pauses—but that analysand had previously been in treatment with a highly interpretive clinician, and I knew she spoke as she did because she anticipated interruptions. It was some time before I realized that this was something very different: Megan did not know that she was speaking out loud. From her perspective she was simply uttering what was crossing her mind, most of which would remain subvocal.

So I was the recipient of the intermittent articulation of what was actually an ongoing process. After some time I would occasionally ask Megan to fill in a few of the blanks, but I soon realized that she was unable to do this. In effect it was like asking her to explain her internal thought process *in situ.*

Instead, we had to live according to an illusion that I understood her.

Thus, even if I did not consciously comprehend what she was saying, I would now and then, within the rhythm of her speaking, say "I see" or "Mmm." This might seem to be disingenuous, but I would never utter such phrases unless I sensed my interjections were appropriate. These comments were not a communication of understanding; rather I think they reflected shared emotional experiences, albeit in a nascent state. Or, as the psychoanalyst Richard Lucas would put it, I was learning to tune in to her "psychotic wavelength."[2]

Over time I became accustomed to this way of being with Megan, so it came as quite a shock when, toward the end of the first year of analysis, she began to speak more clearly. An urgent matter in her personal life required that she seek my understanding of a specific crisis, so I listened and made some comments. She found this helpful, and we began a new phase of the analysis in which she spoke to me more directly. Her free associations included prepositions, and she developed a coherent syntax.

Later she told me that in the beginning she forgot I was actually there. She added that she did not think of herself as being there either. At that time I noticed that only rarely did she use the first person pronoun "I," and it would be uttered in a rather surprising way, as if she were ejecting it.

Once she started to speak more normally, her "I" became softer, more integrated, and she retained this. She explained it to me: "I don't think I have been here all these years, just images and words and feelings passing through my mind. My mind was here . . . but I was not. Does that make sense to you?" It did, and I was struck immediately by the directness of her question. She went on: "I think it was okay my being like this. I was not uncomfortable. It helped that you never asked a question and that you could be silent forever without intruding. There was no difference between my speaking and you listening. It felt as if you were here and not here at the same time." I added, "And as if *you* were here and not here at the same time?" She paused and said, "I didn't know that then, but looking back, that's about right."

Megan evolved in the analysis. She remained somewhat odd, but the fragmented self that came to see me no longer felt broken.

Like most every schizophrenic I have known, she would let me in on a few secrets from her world, almost as if it was a gift in return for my patience. She said she found not feeling much easier than feeling, and after some time she told me why. She said that at the point when she had begun to lose a sense of herself as she knew it—and when she became averse to speaking as an I—the world was impacting on her in new and profound ways. She would see ordinary colors as extraordinarily vivid, and while it was initially intriguing, she soon found it too much. Sounds were either inaudible or much too loud—usually the latter.

Megan dealt with these phenomena in the way anyone might under those circumstances. She would try to avoid people, places, and situations that would increase the likelihood of overly vivid visual experiences or disturbing sounds. She tried to block out her peripheral vision and canalized her line of sight so that objects no longer emerged with distinct colors. She also numbed her hearing so she was rather cut off and heard little.

Ordinarily one thinks of the psychoanalytic session as having a highly structured setting and process: forty-five to fifty minutes each, four or five times a week, using a couch; the patient speaking, the analyst listening and offering occasional interpretations.

Underlying this, however, there is a much less structured dimension. Analysts get lost in their patients' internal worlds; they are guided unconsciously by their free associations, moved by inexplicable emotional experiences, and shaped by the other's character forms. And in some senses this makes the analyst an ideal partner for the schizophrenic, accepting her world for what it is, and how it is. The analyst will never understand fully where he has been, what he has done or not done, what he has learned or forgotten, or where the process is going, but it is precisely the absence of such direction that is suited to the rudderless world of the psychotic. That said, by tolerating this profoundly ambiguous situation the patient and the analyst may emerge out of the partnership having experienced a relationship that proves deeply generative for both.

Jordan, a paranoid schizophrenic, had been in hospital for some months when he was referred to me. He was under five feet tall and seemed like an impish boy, except there was something rather feral about him. He was unsettling.

He had alarmed his colleagues in the office where he worked because he told them he was going to set himself on fire. He brought a lighter to work, and made a small pile of newspapers on his desk; the police were called, and he was hospitalized. A family friend asked if I would see him on the day of his release, and I agreed. We talked for a while, and we arranged that I would take him into analysis five times a week.

I will not detail the course of the treatment but instead concentrate on one feature.

Jordan did not know why he was building the fire. A voice told him to do it, and he was just following instructions. In the first years of the analysis he would hear voices during the session, and I would ask him to take his time and let me know what he was hearing. He was suspicious—one voice would instruct him not to speak to me—but I treated his voices with great respect, and I think this allowed him to be cooperative.

At a certain point I told him that I too spoke to myself, and gave him examples: "You forgot to hand in your license renewal form"; "I wonder what I'll have for dinner tonight." For about a week we swapped voices. He would tell me what he had heard, and I would do the same.

Jordan's most frequent voice was a deeply persecutory one. It would say to him, "You smell." Once day he told me that he would be riding on a bus and the voice would say, "You smell. Get off this bus right now!" or "The person in the seat ahead of you is beginning to smell you," and Jordan would break out into a sweat.

Around this time, in his free associations he harked back to his fire-starting threat. I asked:

"What do you suppose you were doing?"
"Well, I was setting up a barbecue."

"You mean you were going to cook something?"

He laughed.

"I hadn't thought of that!"

"You might not have thought about it *consciously*, but if you had set up a barbecue then what would you have cooked for your colleagues?"

"Kebabs."

"Oh. So if you had had your wish, you would have cooked for your fellow workers and treated them to a first-class meal."

He laughed again.

"Well, of course that's silly. No such thing could happen."

"On the contrary, you just tried to make the meal happen in the wrong place. Couldn't you have invited people to your house for a meal?"

"I'm too shy. And anyway the voices wouldn't allow it."

"So you did the next best thing: by trying to light the fire you were indicating what you wanted to do, but it was not understood."

I then made a leap.

"You know, your voice says 'you smell' and you are haunted by this, but what if you smell like a cook?"

He laughed and laughed. After the amusement, I said: "We know that you are lonely." (I knew he never talked to anyone but me.) "But one way to make friends would be to cook for them. When the voice was telling you that you were smelling in the bus, perhaps you were thinking unconsciously about how to make friends, by cooking for them. But you are so afraid of being in touch with people that a voice ridicules you for what is a basic human wish: to get to know people."

Some interpretations are of interest to a patient; some are not. A few, for whatever reason, seem to become transformational. Two weeks later Jordan came to a session with a small carton. It contained kebab, rice, and lentils. It came with a fork, and he said it was for me. I opened it and ate. I can still see the smile on his face. I told him it was delicious and then risked a joke: "Listen, if this is the way you smell on a bus, those passengers are lucky!"

Jordan did not go on to achieve a robust social life. He remained generally reclusive, but he did form friendships with three people, who in turn helped him meet others. The voices that had taunted him for giving off an odor stopped. It was, in my view, the interpretation of their unconscious intentions that was responsible for removing them from his mind. He knew now that they signified his wish to make contact with people through cooking, which, incidentally, was the primary means for socializing for people in his native land.

During these years of private practice I came to learn that, provided the psychoanalyst has plenty of time to work with a psychotic person and provided the analyst firmly believes that all apparently odd behaviors contain a discernible logic, a way can be found to talk to psychotic people—on their own terms.

But what happens when someone becomes schizophrenic?

7

Mind-Blowing Thoughts

A TWELVE-YEAR-OLD BOY, while sitting in his classroom, hears a voice say, "Your mother won't be at home today." He is startled and shocked, not only by what is said but by an unknown voice speaking this to him. Months go by before the voice returns, again while in class. "Your bottom is showing." Humiliated, he immediately gets up and goes to the loo to check his belt and assure himself that he is not showing his bottom. Within a year the voice appears more frequently and then is accompanied by other distinctive voices. They speak in short, sharp sentences: "Stop!"; "Retie your shoes, now!"; "Twist your nose three times!"

Often the young schizophrenic will tell friends that he or she is having odd ideas, but more likely will choose to slightly illustrate them by demonstrating what appears to be idiosyncratic behavior. Maybe this can all be laughed off?

For example, a fifteen-year-old male thought he should collect stones, put them in a circle in his room, and sit there for some hours chanting poetry by Yeats. A voice had not told him to do this, but he had felt a strange, urgent, and almost excited connection to large rocks near his house. He felt they might be trying to say something to him.

So he invited his friends over for "rock and roll" lessons. His friends joined him for a while. It seemed amusing; offbeat, not a big deal.

Friends will often take note of such idiosyncratic actions and usually join in, but as time goes on—and it might take a few years—the eccentric actions become more and more bizarre, until the schizophrenic begins to hide these thoughts from friends, resorting to false self-communications in the hope that these do not upset others.

Slow-onset schizophrenia is characterized by occasional startling moments in which a person—usually in adolescence—finds himself having strange ideas. They come and go, and indeed many months may pass in the interval of disconcerting ideas.

Those on the verge of schizophrenia may experience profound changes in their way of seeing, hearing, and thinking. Early shocks may include an odd vividness of certain colors that can become eidetic or dreamlike in their intensity. This may be accompanied by an unusual sensitivity to sound. They may hear people talking from afar, or react to an ordinary noise as if it were an explosion. As with the increasingly eccentric actions, they will usually seek to keep such experiences secret. They will have no idea what is happening to them and will not wish to worry friends, but there is also a fear that if they reveal what is taking place it will make matters worse.

As we shall discuss later, this fear of telling others what is going on in the mind, though understandable, is a fateful misjudgment, because it means that in a crucial hour of need, one does not ask for help. Often, those suffering will be high-functioning, charming, sociable people, and the last thing they can imagine is telling a close friend: "I am being taken over by something."

Those who know the person will detect striking changes in his manner of being. He may become withdrawn, or cryptic in what he says, sometimes laughing as if at a private joke. His body gestures may become a means of expressing thoughts. He may move differ-ently: jerking, as if grabbed by invisible beings or trying to avoid them, or sliding along rather than walking, or suddenly halting a ges-ture as though frozen in midair. He may look at his hands for long periods of time or rub his arm or leg as if polishing some precious object. He might stand very still, gazing out a window, apparently oblivious to the presence of others and seeming to take no notice of what is happening around him.

Body change—the way the person moves and gestures—is a very important feature of this alteration of the self. I think the schizophren-ic's relation to his body indicates that the I—the speaker of being—has departed. What remains is purely automatic body knowledge—the person knows how to open a door, sit in a chair, or shake hands—and actions become android-like. This substitution for the human dimen-sion is a crucial aspect of the schizophrenic's voyage.

The other type of onset is distinct and acute. It may happen in a matter of hours, but it usually occurs over a few days before there is a catastrophic breakdown.

A twenty-year-old university student who has never knowingly suffered from any odd psychological experiences wakes up one morn-ing and feels that the room is tilting. She cannot stand properly and decides to crawl on her hands and knees. She then feels that some-thing is removing her vital organs, and she hears the phrase "and now for the liver," whereupon she screams. She screams and screams and soon her roommates have called the police, and she is hospitalized.

The wider impact of a sudden breakdown deserves special atten-tion, as it is so often overlooked. A catastrophic break with reality of course involves a break with family, loved ones, friends, colleagues. The response of the other "performs" a vital part of this breakdown, as the other not only experiences the shock of this difference but also feels a type of loss, grief, and eventually mourning, which is all the more powerful because the schizophrenic person seems utterly oblivious to these side effects.

Others find themselves in a very strange place. We see the person suddenly change before our eyes into someone unfamiliar, increasingly alien. Language starts to be used in disturbing ways. We feel that our presence is negated, but that at the same time we ourselves are having some strange effect on the person that we cannot address or modify. It is as if he is gradually leaving our world; although still present, he has transported himself across some unseen line, crossing over into another reality that totally absorbs his attention.

I believe that the *schizophrenic effect* is intrinsic to this new psychotic being. How do we understand this? Does it not feel like the most profound rejection of our being and the terms of our social life?

Our type of mourning is unique as we are left holding the remnants of the person's former being. What we see is foreign to us and we grieve over the loss of the person we knew. As we talk with him we look for signs of the familiar self, and now and then we see in his eyes some recognition of this. Then he is gone again, subsumed into his psychosis.

Is there any way we can understand this change in terms of human intersubjectivity? Is our loss, our anguish, our frustration a part of this person's loss that cannot be represented? What does he see in those around him, those closest to him, his others? Does he not see the reflection of his own death, the loss of his own being, his own anguish, projected into them? And why would this be happening? What possible reason could there be for the social event we label as the arrival of schizophrenia?

In ordinary circumstances when someone goes missing, disappears from material reality, there is the registration of physical loss. The other might notice that the person has not been seen for some time. His car is found abandoned. Friends and family come to accept that he has gone, perhaps permanently. The schizophrenic's disappearance, on the other hand, is committed before our very eyes. And although this violent action can mean many things, the reaction of others certainly functions as a reflection of the act of disappearance.

Generally speaking, when clinicians take a person with schizophrenia into analytic treatment, we have not known them before the onset of the illness, and in that sense we cannot be witness to this disappearance of the self in the same way as those who are close to them. However, people who work intensively with schizophrenics, especially in a residential setting, do see their idiom of being disappear, again and again. Now and then, if only for a few seconds, the person will revert to his former self. He will make eye contact, we hear a lucid statement of his predicament, we note the change in his body— and then we watch him slip back into the psychotic self.

Slow-onset schizophrenia, if noticed by parents, may lead them to refer their child for intense psychotherapy or psychoanalysis. If this happens, there is a very good chance that the adolescent will not have a full-on schizophrenic breakdown; indeed, it can be reversed and the self returned to something like an ordinary course of life.

Clinicians around the world who have taken adolescents into intensive psychotherapy know this is true. Of course, precisely *because* the schizophrenic process has been encountered and generatively transformed, this ordinary accomplishment has not received the attention it deserves.

It is crucial that psychotherapists and family members or friends of young schizophrenics (as well as the schizophrenics themselves) understand that *if* the young person gets into regular therapy (four or five times a week) *before* the outbreak of a full schizophrenic breakdown, then often the schizophrenia can be remediated and the individual can proceed on his or her way in life. To be sure, that person will always remember the schizophrenic experiences, and even if the anxiety over their appearance is hugely diminished, the memories will remain in the background, generating a low level of fear that they might one day return. How could it be otherwise?

David, a young man in his mid-twenties, looked at me warily. I had asked him how he knew that something crucial in him had changed. He was silent for a while, and then said, "When the sun burst."

One day at school, when he was ten, he ran out of his classroom at break time and suddenly felt that something was different. He looked up, and the sun burst. He ran back into the building and hid in a closet. He could not be found for some hours, and when he was the teachers were very cross with him. How could he pull a trick like this?

He did not know what they were talking about. He told them they were all in danger. He screamed for help and ran, and they chased after him.

For David this was a defining moment. He knew he had seen the sun burst. It was impossible that they had not seen this; it could only be that they were lying to him. Why would they do that? It must be because they were in cahoots with the forces that burst the sun. So he had to shut himself up, remain still. He did this for ten years, until his next schizophrenic "episode."

What does David teach us?

Let's pursue one line of thought.

Life is normal until the apocalypse. Even if the signs of catastrophe seem mild—a feeling of being out of place, but it passes, the impression of hearing voices, the sense that something has entered the body—the schizophrenic will never forget those first experiences.

Mind-Blowing Thoughts

Some process seems to be altering the self without any conscious choice involved in the mutation.

After these shocks, everything changes. The world is not the same; people are no longer safe. But the rest of humanity seems oblivious. In schizophrenia, unlike other psychotic distresses, there are usually a number of these apocalyptic moments in which the person's world view is changed.

Paula told me it happened to her in the sixth grade. She was sitting behind a boy she did not like. One day he told her she had farted, and he mocked her in front of their classmates. From that moment on, every time she saw him, he appeared strangely ugly and metamorphic. One day she looked closely at his ears. They grew. In a matter of seconds they were five times larger than before—they were elephant ears! She was afraid he had some disease that would spread and contaminate her, and she ran out of the room in alarm.

When asked why she had run off, she explained all this to the teacher, expecting some action to be taken. Their lives could be at risk. But no one did anything. She was asked to take her seat behind the boy. After that she never saw the rest of his body, only his ears.

One of the remarkable aspects of schizophrenia is how adaptive people are. Imagine what it is like to be in this place, living in a world that is now changing its shape. One possible response is to transform it into a mythic world, and to reconstruct one's being into a transcendent muse who can control this.

As we saw in the case of Paula and her classmate, schizophrenics can transform their perception of the object world so that their anxieties are represented by distortion in the size of an object. (Interestingly, we see a similar device used in pre-Renaissance paintings, where, for example, the significance of the Virgin Mary was emphasized by depicting her as much larger than the ordinary mortals who surrounded her.)

I learned from the children at EBAC that another inventive solution is to transform human others into cartoon figures or caricatures that represent particular characteristics or qualities. So one person might embody care, another defense, another joy, another menace. People are thus reduced to a psychological principle: we are no more than that which we are chosen to embody, figures of the *allegorical imaginary*. (Before we label this too readily as a bizarre representation of others, we might think of how ordinary stereotyping and gossip are similar ways of tagging selves with virtues or vices.)

The assigning of qualities in this way can have complex consequences. If a certain person embodies the quality "safety," the schizophrenic may need to touch her physically a set number of times per day, or at least be in her vicinity in order to be safe. On the other hand, being near someone who embodies, for example, "bad memories" will be dangerous, so he may need to turn his back every time that person walks by. We can see how the dehumanization that has taken place within the schizophrenic is projected into the other, who now serves simply as a vessel for some part of the self. This is a form of *schizophrenic ritualization;* the person now inhabits an intense, allegoric world in which relationships are displaced by ritualized encounters.

A contented self accepts the social order. It believes in the hegemonic harmonics of social synchrony. We all sing together; there are no discordant voices. But if the schizophrenic is to participate in the social order he must resort to an ancient illusion: that we can protect the self against primordial harm (any form of danger that threatens the existence of the self). Schizophrenia operates in inverse proportion to self-fulfillment. In the schizophrenic order, a self fulfilled is a self endangered. But a self intelligently emptied is a self protected.

Primordial harm, whether in the real or in the mind, causes him to retreat into primitive defenses in order to protect the true self from annihilation. The threat may come from a voice: "If you think of sex you will explode and your blood and bones will scatter everywhere." This is a form of endopsychic interruption from the depths of the mind. Schizophrenics do not want to receive these messages. They often regard themselves as unfortunate seers or sages, tasked with reporting the message so that humanity can be saved.

By reducing human beings to an allegoric corollary, the schizophrenic aims to preserve some connection with others while at the same time projecting parts of the self into the object world. He therefore fills the object world with allegorical objects and rituals that enable him to negotiate his social existence in relative safety.

One curious form of schizophrenic defense is the transformation of lived experience into applied literature. Unable to bear the uncertain nature of live company, a schizophrenic may secretly transform others into figures in a narrative. The surrounding world becomes a book that can be controlled by moving it page by page. We might see him scanning the room as if he were reading it, maybe making a particular sound as he mimes turning a page. I recall one patient who would say "ka-ching" and close his eyes emphatically each time he moved his gaze from one sector of the visual field to another.

Why would he do this?

By transforming his field of vision into a booklet, he aimed to rid life of its unpredictable nature. The self, removed as a participant, becomes a reader. Others are reduced to illustrations of themselves or to qualities their character embodies.

(Why "ka-ching"? Because, as I was later informed, it is the sound of a cash register, and each view of his world was accounted for by cashing it in.)

At the same time, however, transforming the world into a text is at least a way of being with people. Being with a physical other also means being inside one's own body, but the embodied self can be an embarrassing container at best and a horrifying implicator at worst. If one is present, one could become involved with other bodies. Many schizophrenics do not know how to relate to others as a free, sentient self, with a receptive unconscious ticking over in each second of life, simply taking the world in. In place of this ordinary, nourishing relation to life, the schizophrenic will often substitute unrelenting conscious thought, weighing up each moment of being, working out how to be in the presence of others and evaluating what to say.

Keeping people at a literary remove is an attempt at a form of compromise between the hallucinatory and the actual. It is a fairly adept solution to a dreadful dilemma.

PART TWO

8

From History to Mythology

DENIS SPENT WEEKS TELLING ME of life before his birth. A huge young man, well over 275 pounds, he looked Buddha-like, especially because he wore loose-fitting clothing and sat legs crossed on the sofa rather than in a chair.

Similar to another patient I had worked with, he felt obliged to describe in meticulous detail his experience as a sperm inside his father, and then the Odyssean journey up the fallopian tube to find the maternal egg. He described the act of insemination as if two life forces met in incandescent destinies. Time as a fetus was a long and rich experience, a prelapsarian world of colors, sounds, intimate movement, and much more. Then, unfortunately, he was born and his heroic journey was destroyed.

About his life after birth he had little to say.

Descriptions of his everyday life were narratives of elemental encounters. His semen-self would commune with natural elements mountains, streams, or the wind—and was possessed of an intelligence that could inseminate relations with others. He could communicate the deep wisdom he possessed or procreate with the elemental in others and give issue to a new understanding of them. Now and then he would offer to show someone what he learned of them. He might, for example, present them with a special leaf, stating that they had a unique bond with that particular tree; that they should visit it and keep the leaf on their person for the sake of this intimacy.

The discrete elements of everyday life may be given a new and allegorical meaning as a schizophrenic battles with forces and adversities that the non-psychotic world would regard as metaphors. He has resolved to leave the world of the ordinary. To become a sage he must of necessity decline the human experience, as everyday life represents a threat to his claim to a transcendent wisdom. He must destroy the historical past in order to create a new self, living in a new world, obedient to encrypted meanings that only he can discover.

As he becomes schizophrenic, a person may transform the collected memories of his past into a mythological narrative in which he assigns to family and childhood veiled meanings that only he—a sage who has encrypted meaning into myth—can reveal. As we know, myths are based in part on selected facts from reality, but by mythologizing the past the schizophrenic shifts the burden of explanation for his being from the pain of actual lived experiences to the new and grandiose realm of an invented past.

When the breakdown occurs, the self loses the function of historicity—the capacity to transform the past into a narrative. The loss of historic capability happens partly because the schizophrenic's mind is no longer capable of this kind of integrative work, and partly because contacting the past is too painful. It is not simply the pain of past events in themselves, although this may be a factor; it is to do with the *relationship* of the self to a past that now seems broken forever. The cumulative impact of visual and auditory hallucinations eliminates the self's contact with his life; indeed, when thinking back he will often imagine horrifying events that never happened. It is best to be without history.

The creation of a mythic self allows for *schizophrenic transcendence* in which one rises above the scene of catastrophe to an alternative reality inhabited by an avatar with an invented past. Schizophrenic transcendence does not eliminate mental pain or terror—the mythic world is inhabited by dangerous voices, visions, and demons—but it does provide the self with some way of structuring its past, present experience, and future.

During this period in the analysis of a schizophrenic, the psychoanalyst may become a sort of cultural anthropologist, attending carefully to the patient's myths. Inside the story of the self's past and the characters that populate this world are encoded memories, both of the self's fantasy life and his actual existence.

Knowledge of what has been stored in *schizophrenic mythology* is important to the third area, in which the schizophrenic's mythic system will live alongside the recollections and interests described by the analyst from his own life. It will also include shared concerns—current hospital issues, perhaps, or the cultural and political situation.

Some are *oscillatory schizophrenics,* living for periods of time in a parallel universe populated by hallucinatory figures and governed by separate axioms of life, before reentering reality. They become accustomed to traveling back and forth between their worlds.

These activities—the eradication of one's history, the invention of a personal mythology, and communion with the thingness of the world—can be floridly disturbing to the other, but at times there is an indescribable sweetness to the occasional schizophrenic inventiveness.

Timing is everything in analytic work, and eventually the moment comes when the analyst will hazard the restoration of the schizophrenic's historicity. This will take the form of identifying simple facts from the patient's life, such as where they went to school. Usually the analyst would avoid asking a question ("Where did you go to high school?"), but he might mention something he knows, for example that the patient went to "Hollywood High." He might then make some detailed statements about the school: "I think it is over on Vine Street, as I recall. And I think it has a rather large auditorium with white curtains and gold lace on them." No pressure should be put on the patient to confirm or deny these facts. The analyst is attempting merely to link the patient to the past as real, instead of the past as a mythic object or a hallucinatory invasion spoken by an internal voice.

If by chance the analyst has happened upon the location of an important projective identification—if Hollywood High is the place where childhood memories are stored—then the patient may respond in a violent way, either verbally or physically. But if the analyst knows the patient very well, he is usually guided by unconscious knowledge not to violate the sanctity of the projective spaces.

This process returns the patient in an undramatic, everyday way to the actual objects of his past. This cannot be achieved, however, unless there has first been a full hearing of the analysand's mythic self. The myths are profound dreams stored throughout the lifetime of the self, and they are precious. The analyst has to accept that these myths may define the work for a long time, and they must be treated with great respect.

Earlier we discussed how in normal life we live in various overlapping collective unconsciouses: family, region, nation, and so forth. As the schizophrenic loses (or rejects) history in favor of mythology, he quietly goes about creating his own collective universe. He does so by forming relationships, not to people, but to things.

He seeks the thingness of things.

He might make a heap of mud and put stones, discarded bottles, or pieces of wood into this highly significant object. This does not in fact represent a collective, although that is the intent. Instead, each of these additions becomes part of an *amalgam*. The object agglomerates differentiated objects and forces them into a mass that has a presumed significance held only in the mind of the schizophrenic.

In a curious objectification of what I term "metasexuality" (a "sexual" unification of mother-father-infant), which I shall discuss in further detail shortly, disparate elements become engaged in frenzied connectedness. At the same time, the schizophrenic's investment in combining things betrays the unconscious effort to move away from people and especially to transcend the intensity of human relations. It is as if the majestic power of sexual pantheism gives way to a semimystical union with inert objects—pieces of metal, dried clay, rocks. The inertness of the object world is appealing precisely because it is immobile; to embrace the inert is to recover from the exhaustions of metasexuality.

Another tactic may be employed to still the movements of the world. In a verbal correlate of this process of concretization, the schizophrenic may "thing" language. Although capable of ordinary speech, he may alter ordinary signifiers, often combining phonemes into neologisms that cancel out meaning. Sentences become syntactical amalgams that are indecipherable, thus protecting the self from the impingement of any potential reply from the other. Collecting objects, whether physical or verbal, is a means of appearing to be part of a group while ensuring that it can have no effect on the self.

As the schizophrenic "things" the world, he reflects the unconscious conviction that he himself is now merely a thing—a human thing that cannot socialize with people, unless it is with others who have become part of the thing-world as an amalgamation. The world of thingness thus becomes the realm of the schizophrenic, who feels that he has special knowledge of the real, that he knows its intrinsic structures and how to work with them and alongside them. He himself

From History to Mythology

is simply a part of the amalgam; indeed, it becomes almost a religious mission to align himself with the thingness of the world. In his meta-sexuality, he has embodied sexual union, and he now presides over what is born from this form of intercourse: a strange combination that reflects his own compromised being. These activities—the eradication of history, the invention of a personal mythology and communion with the thingness of the world—can often be florid and highly disturbing to the other, but they may also be very subtle indeed.

9

Leaving Things Alone

THOSE WHO WORK WITH schizophrenics describe *schizophrenic presence,* which they experience as being with someone who has seemingly crossed over from the human world to the non-human environment. It can be an eerie and uncomfortable feeling. People who had known the schizophrenic before their breakdown find themselves encountering what seems like the self's bizarre double. We witness a splitting of the self: a negative transformation giving birth to a psychotic self, emerging from the destruction of the former subject.

The person "on the other side" is almost a caricature of human life. Ordinary everyday gestures may become mechanical. When the schizophrenic reaches for a cup of coffee, we often see a person in tensile slow motion, the torso moving first as if corseted by some hidden metal fabric; the shoulders and arms operate in curious opposition to one another as if the person is reaching both toward and away from the object at the same time. The cup is approached as if it were dangerous. He might take five minutes to take the first sip and seem to derive no pleasure from drinking. Instead he might blink rapidly or abruptly push the cup away as if attacked by the object.

What we see is a robotic self, one that appears to have no originating subjectivity, no interior. Drinking a cup of coffee may be accomplished in painful slow motion, each inch of the total action seeming to have been programmed by a computer. The schizophrenic also communicates the sense that the object has animistic potential.[1] So, while the self seems mechanical, the cup is approached as if it were alive and might spring into some unforeseen action. This conviction is rarely voiced by the schizophrenic, but it is uttered through the tacit language of the body.

The clinician might find himself with the bizarre thought that the cup might suddenly go flying across the room. He starts to feel afraid of ordinary objects, as if they could become violent. Is this simply concern that the patient may throw the object, or drop it? The clinician is not sure. It is the sheer uncertainty of the status of the self vis-à-vis the object that is experienced in these moments. We see here how the patient creates a *schizophrenic atmosphere,* in which the clinician finds himself with a strange anxiety about safety in the ordinary world.

More often than not, however, what we see in residential settings is something quite different. We see staff members who are unnaturally calm. They move in slow motion, they speak simply and deliberately, they smile a lot and look into their patients' eyes with a doe-eyed gaze.

This is an extreme response to living in the schizophrenic atmosphere. The clinician feels rather like an astronaut walking on a foreign planet. His insistent calm defends the self against the incursion of the irrational anxiety that the non-human object world has a dangerous animistic potential.

When this calm breaks down it can be startling. I once watched a therapist who had been sitting for some twenty minutes next to a mute schizophrenic. She was deep into her counterpsychotic calm when, by "accident," the schizophrenic nudged a magazine off the arm of the sofa, whereupon the therapist jumped up with such force that she banged into a coffee table, launched herself into space, and fell on her face. The patient did not seem to notice, but the therapist was clearly very upset and disoriented. As she excused herself and left the room I saw a smile cross the patient's face.

What was he smiling about? We shall never know. But it seems reasonable to assume that, for a moment, he had brought about in his therapist the kind of terror that he felt about ordinary objects. We can see that the therapist jumped up, not because the magazine itself was dangerous, but because its sudden movement embodied the potential movement of the patient. He was the magazine. As it fell, so could he. But as it fell so did the therapist. She experienced first hand the frightening world on the other side; a world of belief (derived from projection) that the object is just barely asleep and could awake at any moment to do something sudden, bewildering, and dangerous.

What the schizophrenic reveals is the hallucinogenic potential of the object world. He has seen the object change its character. It cannot be trusted. His dehumanization and transformation of self into the mechanical is a protective measure; objects come alive to destroy the human, but the self cannot be damaged if it is not there to begin with.

Those clinicians who react to the patient with unreal calm are unconsciously, and rather astutely, meeting the patient halfway. Both persons are unreal and rendezvous in a kind of neutral territory. There are no strong affects. Observations are of a very simple kind. Speech is slowed down, language laundered of color. If clinicians were to behave like this in any other circumstance, they would seem very disturbed indeed. What they are doing, however, is attempting to operate in an intermediate area between the psychotic and the non-psychotic world. With the aim of being completely unthreatening, the clinician has transformed herself into an impossibly benign form of being, an exoskeleton of the human.

As we have seen, the human element has been projected into the object world that has become animistic, and may be awakened from its slumber by any sudden motion. The wise therapist is one who knows how to bring an outline of the human into view without waking up the terrifying objects. In time—and this may mean years—the clinician will hope to convince the patient that his being is not the container of hidden violence, rapaciously deranged sexuality, or bizarre thought disorders. The clinician's false self becomes a transitional experience for the schizophrenic, enabling him to move from the safety of the non-human object world to experience the dangers of the human realm.

10

Metasexuality

SOME SCHIZOPHRENICS MAY express a feeling that they have a special connection to both the animate and the inanimate world (to trees, rivers, buses, roads), and they may also feel that the self has undergone multiple psychic mitoses. Such a person has entered into the world of polarities (male and female, mother and father, animate and inanimate), and he speaks now as an integrated assembly of opposites.

He proposes that he is engaged in a form of constant intercourse with, and between, objects—a theory I term *metasexuality*.

"Meta": beyond. Metasexuality: transcending sexuality.

Schizophrenic metasexuality aims to eliminate the disturbing psychic effects of the primal scene by incorporating it, and all of its unconscious derivatives, thereby nullifying the reality of sexuality altogether. This is achieved, paradoxically, by omnisciently treating *all* connections in life—person to person, a person to an idea, an object to any other object—as sexual. By sexualizing everything, the schizophrenic proactively eradicates the specificity of erotic fantasy life and the reality of sexual engagement with a specific other.

Actual sexual life is nullified by a democratization of the word to the point of its vanishing into insignificance.

Why does the schizophrenic resort to this particular solution?

Mothers and fathers differ, and that difference is hard for children to bear. One solution they adopt is the elimination of this duality. In the fantasy life of the child, when the parents make love they become "the beast with two backs." In the child's mind sexuality is not simply an intercourse, it is a moment when two sexes blend into a single entity.

In schizophrenia this fantasy takes on a different and more extended form. The schizophrenic will display a type of bisexuality in which he assumes that he is both male and female, as if by eradicating these differences and reassembling them within his own personality organization he has transcended them. This may be seen as an alternative solution to the ordinary Oedipal complex. By becoming both mother and father, through combining them and subsuming them into his own self, he triumphs over parental authority. In infancy and early toddlerhood the parents' voices both are and are not part of the internal world, both are and are not identifiable. It may be that the auditory hallucinations of the schizophrenic are echoes of maternal and paternal voices, angry at being trumped in this manner.

However, there are other aspects to metasexuality. In its manic transcendence of the Oedipal triangle, the self believes it is controlling not only the act of sexual intercourse but also any "births" that emanate from this. The self is now felt to connect all objects in continual acts of metaphysical union. The fantasy of incorporating parental intercourse is an attempt to forestall and control the regressions occurring in the mind by resorting to the most powerful internal means. The mania of sexual omnipotence aims to re-situate a failing self within a position of power, but ironically this is a position derived

from the very phenomenology of regression itself, as adult perceptions and experiences are pocked by infantile percepts.

The result is a divided self, split in two, but with the infantile and
adult parts of the personality also existing in parallel. The schizophrenic has joined two eras and two selves into one and has evoked
the power of sexuality to accomplish this defense.

However, he believes that there are higher forms of intercourse
than mere sexual union. By incorporating sexuality, and thereby neu-
tralizing it, the schizophrenic feels he has attained a higher realm of
intercourse in which attracting opposites are combined into new
forms of bliss, which are sometimes experienced as intense spiritual
communions.

This can sometimes take forms that, to the rest of us, may seem
amusing or absurd.

For example, a schizophrenic may cook a meal of broccoli and
sliced socks. The sock may be cooked for a long time and seasoned
with various spices before the broccoli is added. The idea is not so
much to enjoy the meal itself, but to bring opposites into a state of
attraction (socks and broccoli are now in a form of intercourse), defying the culinary gods and declaring the self a new deity that presides
over the hitherto irreconcilable.

Lacan makes a seminal distinction in his theory of psychosis. He
maintains that the psychotic refuses the Symbolic order and collapses
into the Imaginary—the preverbal mentational world of the infant
self. In my view, the schizophrenic who unconsciously employs metasexuality as a solution is operating at a manic level, as the controller
of both the Imaginary and Symbolic orders. By achieving this form
of transcendence, he controls the universe of imagination and speech.
When the listener is confounded by his articulations, this only con-
firms his manic sense of superiority. He oscillates back and forth

between image-thinking and linguistic representation, between body language (primal scene representation) and gesture; conforming to the laws of grammar and then tearing them up, rearranging syntax as an act in itself. He is constantly engaged in this movement between two worlds, between the infantile and the post-verbal selves, pseudo-parented by an incorporated parental sexuality.

Metasexuality is therefore a schizophrenic object relation based on a manic conviction that the subject has triumphed over and incorporated the mother and father and become a we-world. By virtue of this expansive action, the subject acquires super powers. Although the body-self feels energized by the appropriation, the act of incorporative triumph desexualizes the primal scene—rather as the digestive system eliminates the taste of food.

Ultimately, "higher" forms of intercourse will be achieved by connecting mental objects rather than physical ones. These may consist of knowledge-based connections between people or specific affinities such as shared musical tastes that can feel more blissful and ecstatic to the schizophrenic than sexual orgasm.

The fact that these connections retain an unconscious sexual basis will generally not be obvious. It is important to our understanding of the complexity of the schizophrenic's sexuality to understand that his excitement at the incorporation of parental intercourse does not involve sexual sensations, and is not related to normal pregenital or genital forms of sexuality. Schizophrenic metasexuality finds bliss in the transcendental incorporative amalgamation of opposites.

However, there are endless problems with this solution. With the regression comes a breakthrough of intense, infantile forms of perception and organization (tactile-kinesthetic, visual, auditory, and so on). The fantasy is compelling and exhausting, as he continually attempts to incorporate the parental primal scene. He is borrowing from its imagined power in order to scaffold a self that is falling to pieces, and matters are made worse by the sense that he has murdered the mother and the father.

He now finds himself in a profoundly solitary position, alone with a terror that the world will take revenge upon him. When he hears voices or encounters objects moving in the real he assumes that he is about to be annihilated for his crimes. This produces an agitation that can build to disturbing states of frenzy, and in extreme situations the mania gives way to a catatonic stupor, which is welcomed as a delibidinalization of the endless metasexualizations.

Let us end this chapter with ten-year-old Larry of EBAC. He illustrates how a schizophrenic child aims to reach sexuality, understood in this chapter as a lordship over the parental intercourse, or what I am terming metasexuality. It bears remembering that Larry would touch other children on the forehead with his index finger and hum, which meant he was going to put them into one of his comic books that day, an event that frightened all of the children who could not distinguish between the imaginary and the actual. He would put his finger in his mouth to wet it before touching a child on the forehead. This was a procreative necessity, as the people he created in his comic book were his offspring. They confirmed this by begging him not to go into the book, but if he touched them on the forehead they were fated to a harrowing experience.

Larry thought of himself as a god. His parents infuriated him because they were "bigger" than him, and he could not figure out why great size had yet to be bestowed on him. He did not think of himself as a child and looked upon sex as that magical something that his parents could do and once he could get hold of it, he would be master of the universe. In his more troubled moments he would cry out, "I am a shrimp!" "I am a shrimp at the bottom of the sea." As absurd as this statement might seem, when we heard Larry say this it immediately drew us to him, because we knew he was in profound despair. As he said this, tears would stream down his cheeks. He would often just crumble on the floor . . . collapsed. He was determined to get away from being a shrimp at the bottom of the sea. He was convinced that he just "had to make it to sex," as he reported one day. By this, I later learned, he meant he had to know how to do it so he could surpass his parents and gain immeasurable power.

11

Hearing Voices

I HAVE DISCUSSED HOW schizophrenics may animate the object
world, which leads them to tread softly in a realm they do not wish to
awaken. This is part of a complex set of anxieties. Another source of
anxiety is panic over loss of the mind. Schizophrenics do not lose the
sense that they exist. They retain a sense of self, but this is a self
vastly changed from its former incarnations, and they experience a
change in the traditional relation between mind and self that most of
us take for granted.

As I discuss later in the book, although the schizophrenic may use
"I" when reporting inner thoughts to the other, it is often highly compromised, as though it has been given an android pronominal function. Something of its freedom is gone. It is more like a distant
reporter, afraid of the world around it, barely able to speak, cowering
before the voices now invading inner space.

At first, often the voices a schizophrenic hears seem to come from
the inanimate object world: a tree speaks, or a stream, or a rock. Then
in time the voices generally become disconnected from the objects
and begin to speak from inside the self's mind. There may be a set of
voices that seem to have independent personalities. Initially some

schizophrenics may try to make friends with them. They will differentiate themselves, as listeners, from the speaking voices and they will often disagree with them, though they may also revere them.

Why is this?

Children often have similar responses, welcoming inanimate or nonhuman objects as companions. Kids love stories about a noble tree or a friendly seaside that welcomes visitors, or about animals like the Velveteen Rabbit. The objects are given human qualities, and children seek friendship in them.

It is part of the remarkable action of schizophrenia that an adult returns to this position, to the infant's perception of the universe: the thingness of objects is vivid, colors feature prominently in the discrimination of percepts, sound is a crucial aspect of the object world, as is movement-in-itself. (An infant will be captivated by watching the movement of objects.) Except that now, for the adult, these strange objects are not so friendly after all. They have the potential to betray the doctrine that if we love one another all will be well. The schizophrenic perceives that the idea that we are benign, well-meaning, and socially constructive is a ponzi scheme of illusions. The schizophrenic has experienced the world differently. And, like an advance party on an expedition that encounters insurmountable challenges, he quickly retreats to base camp.

When the self's integrity is threatened with annihilation, we immediately act to preserve ourselves, and the I may be sequestered, put into a place of hiding. It may be projected for safekeeping into stand-ins or proxies in order to fool anyone who might be trying to find it and destroy it. So a schizophrenic might lodge his true self in a tree, a rock, or a brook. When these speak to him, he is speaking to himself in their voices. The fact that they are safeguarding this true self explains why he reveres them, for they know he is in trouble and their instructions are attempts at helping him.

The voices will almost always be at odds with the politics of the world at large. They may tell him to do strange things—he must hopscotch all the way home or walk only on the edge of the pavement—but the fact that onlookers are alarmed by such behavior only affirms that his I is giving him correctly evasive instructions that will fool the forces seeking to destroy him. Such movements can of course be over-determined. Viewed in the context of schizophrenic metasexuality, jumping from one place to another may also be an unconscious representation of the movements of intercourse. The I is now hiding itself in the we-world of triadic sexuality, as the self merges into the figures of mother and father locked in a sexual frenzy that gives birth to a new creature there and then.

Some schizophrenics report later that they experienced the voices as highly dangerous and frightening from the beginning and feared their arrival. These voices are usually judging the self harshly or issuing instructions to commit antisocial actions. Unsurprisingly, how the voices sound and what they say will be based on the person's prior mentality, on his ways of thinking about the world and, particularly, on the way he has talked to the self since early childhood. If he has a harsh conscience, then the voices may tend to be violent. If he has been less judgmental of himself, the voices may feel friendlier.

Indeed, the voices originate from distinct parts of the child self. Certain events in the child's experience of reality may have been too painful or too puzzling to contemplate and were repudiated. The events, and the parts of the self that experienced them, were cast out of mind. Since they were ejected by the self, they are not part of the person's conscious sense of his history, so when they return later in the form of voices they seem to speak from the outside, as if they are foreign to the self. However, if these split-off parts of the self have been valued—a love of friendship, for example—then that repudiated portion of the self may return as a friendly voice that feels loving, rather like an imaginary companion.

But however the voices are experienced at the start, the honeymoon with the projected I will generally last only a few months before the demands become increasingly exhausting and impossible. This does not mean belief in the voices will be abandoned as a crucial functioning part of the self, but faith in their wisdom will diminish.

In their plurality, the voices that now contain the function of the I are existentially closer to the truth than our "normal" illusion of unitary mental status. The fact is that the I has never been a unified perspective but has always represented many differing views. We are heterogeneous, full of contradictions; our views and self-advice may be either sound or self-deluding.

From a structural point of view, the illusory hegemony of the I is challenged by the intrusion of the voices, and the self is therefore forced to try to banish them. Even as a schizophrenic tries to listen to the wisdom seemingly inherent in these voices, the grammar of the internal dialogue presents their views as coming from an other who speaks to the self, and they are therefore excluded from participation in the subjective being.

Another way to think of this is that the illusion of controlling the parental sexual scene wanes as the world fails to accord with the self's demands. Things don't go the schizophrenic's way, and with shocks to his sense of omnipotence come fears that if he is not in control of this experiment then he is at the mercy of the forces he had presumed to incorporate. What will happen if the we-world throws off his dominance and seeks retaliation?

Of interest, as well, is the intrasubjective sensation of the spatial *position* of the voices. Some seem very far removed, as though speaking from a great distance. Others seem close, loud, and demanding.

Whereas a normal person speaks silently to the self, the schizophrenic will report the voices as actual sounds with distinct vocal characteristics. The proximity, the sound and character of the voices, whether they are single or multiple—all these aspects create the strange situation of being a witness to the self's own mental life. As he returns to the child's space as a child-adult hybrid, he is split between these two positions. And a fragment of the self is able to witness this odd happening, enabling the self to possess the illusion (correct, in a sense) that it sees more than anyone else into the mysteries of the mind.

Bion, and others, would attribute this observational ability to the "non-psychotic" parts of the personality. A problem with this formulation, however, is that although all schizophrenics do retain non-psychotic areas of functioning, at no point are they disconnected from a guiding unconscious fantasy that the self is immersed in the we-world of metasexuality. They pluralize their subjective experience, repeatedly encountering new forms of intercourse between objects that they then attempt to incorporate and control. Meeting new people, encountering new places, are all experienced as excitements that must be assimilated into the self.

It is important to emphasize again that this form of sexuality is almost entirely unconscious. The aim is not to generate sexual excitation leading to an orgasmic conclusion, but to connect all objects through sexual libido, utilizing the sense of fusion intrinsic to sexual excitement in order to bind objects under the spell of the excitation. The self will not betray such feelings, but this type of manic state exudes a pantheistic bliss.

In the early stages the schizophrenic's mind will tend to take him away from the everyday world. While talking about going to the supermarket, for example, he might be thinking about asteroids headed toward earth, then about how this can be reversed, then on to ever more complex realms of thought. Increasingly out of touch with those around him, he finds it harder to concentrate on what is being said as ideas become incrementally intrusive.

As schizophrenia takes hold, the person splits into different temporal selves (infant, child, adolescent, adult). The various ideas that form part of his mental wanderings may now be delegated to different voices, leaving the I as a lone speaker in an assembly dominated by a cacophony of competing speakers who are ruthless in the pursuit of unknown agendas. Gradually he develops the conviction that the mind is in danger and must be protected.

This sense will often be derived from what he experiences as implicit instructions from objects and the external world—a wind coming up, dark clouds moving across the sky, a black cat crossing his path. In other words, a sign system replaces signification. These assigned meanings often originate in rather ordinary ways: dark clouds bring rain, water makes you wet. These direct relations to the real gradually usurp the signifying function of the mind, however; the self increasingly believes in the link between the sign system and the sense system, losing the capacity for abstraction and reverting to a kind of Lockean view of life. So, a car may be a sign of removal to hospital, and the sight of a car might induce panic and rage; a pen might have become the sign for a negative written comment on the self in the past, and therefore induce anxiety in the present.

At this point, the task of the therapist is to ask after these voices without judging them. One approach—to reason with the patient, explaining that the voices do not make sense—is unlikely to be effective, as it ignores the mental reality that the voices are the self in disguise. It is best simply to listen to what each voice is saying and to ask for further details. This type of questioning accomplishes a rather ironic therapeutic effect. The voices are used to speaking out of the blue. They issue instructions—"Don't listen," "Don't answer"—but they do not usually carry on a conversation with the self.

Most important, the voices cannot free-associate. They cannot respond to a simple request to hear more of what they mean. So the schizophrenic may turn to them for further guidance or elaboration, but this will not be forthcoming. This puts the analyst and the patient in the same boat: what are they to make of what has been said? It is now a question of *translating* the comment into something sensible and, as this takes place, the sequestered functional position of the voice is undermined by the patient's increasing use of the I function. This is an inevitable outcome of getting the analysand to talk, and it is profound. One does not have to ask the patient to give up the voices; one simply has to treat them with dignity and ask him to help the clinician understand what they mean. Eventually the thinker can return to take possession of the thoughts.

In time he cannot escape the question: if these voices are really so wise and their edicts are to be obeyed at all costs, why are they incapable of elaborating their points of view? Schizophrenics are often highly intelligent, literate people, so the failure of these otherwise revered voices to expand on their oracular pronouncements begins to diminish their significance. Eventually they become rather tedious and predictable. Their power diminishes, not because someone has reasoned with the schizophrenic to think differently but because the voices have lost their intellectual credibility.

The voices do speak, however, for split-off parts of the self linked with important experiences that for one reason or another were banished from the mind. Usually it is only a matter of time before such repudiated fragments of self will return. However, if the psychologist listens to a voice, discovers what this part of the self is saying, and takes the core message seriously, then the fury of the voice will diminish as its message is received.

Voices may no longer be speaking for a specific self-state, but are representing instead the *effect* of being split off. It is as if the messenger now speaks, not for the split-off content, but for the fact of being banished. Embedded in the voice's anger is a profound grief over the loss of that part of the self's participation in being. When this happens, the voice is no longer trying to convey a specific view with the potential to be discovered and understood, but is railing against the world, perpetually attacking the self in an endless expression of rage and mental pain.

It is possible to discuss a voice with a schizophrenic, but it is much more difficult to talk about a visual hallucination. Indeed, visual hallucinations are a rarity in schizophrenia, even if in the public imagination this is the notion of how a schizophrenic sees the world. It remains to be seen in future clinical studies of schizophrenics whether hearing voices is a compromise, in which the self unconsciously selects intrusive voices rather than succumbing to intrusive hallucinations.

To hear a voice inside the mind—even if it is not a familiar voice—is to entertain the familiar. To hallucinate during the day is not a familiar phenomenon. Daydreams are hallucinations, but they are carefully segregated from the auspices of consciousness, which successfully negates them as troubling.

So we may ask whether to hear a voice is to hang on to the symbolic order rather than to drown in the dissolving chaos of the imaginary order in which images—one after the other in hallucinated selection—annihilate that perceptual coherence that we associate with the seat of consciousness.

12

Assumed Knowledge

ONE DAY AT EBAC I HAD a bit of a struggle—or learning experience, if you like—with a Japanese-American kid called Ido. He would always say, "Ido wants . . ."; he never used the first person. So for a few days I said, "Ido, it is okay for you to say 'I want a cookie.'" But he would reply, "Ido wants a cookie!" Eventually it became clear that when I suggested he might say "I want," he heard this as an instruction for him to say that I, Christopher, wanted the cookie. He therefore thought I was trying to take away his cookie.

For about a week I transcribed his speech, and I offer one sample here. Ido talking:

> Watch Friday drama. Theatre on KTVU San Francisco–
> Oakland.   Watch   Saturday drama theatre on KTVU
> San Francisco–Oakland. Get in there!   Watch it! Channel 2
> take a bath. Kellogg's Sugar Frosted Flakes,   Kellogg's
> Corn Flakes. Kellogg's Rice Krispies. Kellogg's Special K.
> Kellogg's Sugar Frosted Flakes. Tony, Robert, pane of glass.
> Ron bang   glass. Bobs's Instant Sparkling Cream. Get in
> there and watch! Watch   Merv Griffin Evening. Andy

Second Season. American Papermate. Takaha. Watch Merv Griffin. Watch James cry. Johnny. Johnny. You burn T.V. Spank Johnny spank. Get going. You can't. John, John, what do you do. Hey John. Get going. Get going. I beat your tail off. Can't watch *Password*. Go away. Get out of this apartment. Go over to Steves House. Evening. Go away. Second Season CBS. KPIX, Stan, TV, is over. Johnny spank

Dumont. KTVU Channel 2. Be still. Yes you did! Yes you did. Johnny spank the TV. KTVU Channel 2—Huck Hound—no, no. Johnny, Channel 2, cry, cry. Mennen 44. The Swing Comedy Daytime Show. CBS. Johnny spank the Dumont. Spank. What are you doing to Bobs? Fix Channel 2 bath, cry, be deaf, death. Channel 2 don't work in the afternoon. Watch Marshall J in the afternoon on KPIX Channel 5. Channel 2 bad, cry. Pat Paulson.

This is how Ido talked most of the time. When he was sitting he would rock back and forth, when walking he would hunch over and speak to the ground. He rarely talked *to* anyone, and if he needed something he would pull at your shirt or try to move you toward an object that he wanted. On rare occasions he would make eye contact, but otherwise he averted his gaze.

Any reader could make certain links from the above example of his dialogue. He was probably watching a lot of television, as he certainly knew the channels and the names of daytime TV hosts. Did he choose to do this, or did his parents or caregivers plop him in front of the TV because he was too hard to handle? Interspersed among the channels there seem to be snippets of conversation directed at him, plus internally directed voices, mostly of a punitive type. The segment "bath, cry, be deaf, death" followed by the "Channel 2 don't work in the afternoon" (which was not true) may have been connected with his distress over having to take a bath, a situation that elicited so much mental pain that for him it was like dying; indeed, even the TV channel that linked him to the world would stop working.

It is not possible, of course, to know whether Ido was silent when he was alone. It may be that such a stream of inner talk, externalized in this way, was intended to be overheard; that he was telling the listener of distress over being bathed. Oftentimes I would comment on those lines of thought that I could discern, but he rarely responded, although on occasion he would suddenly stop and look at me for a few seconds before resuming his rocking and speaking. One time I made the disastrous decision to repeat his talking back to him. I did not see it coming when he hit me on the side of the head and knocked me to the ground. I certainly never tried that again.

Ido's use of language illustrates a radical avoidance of linguistic subjectivity. However, in order to understand a rather more subtle aspect of the schizophrenic's relation to his own self, it is helpful to make a distinction between "I" and "me." Others, notably George Herbert Meade and William James, have made a similar differentiation, but I shall be using these terms in my own particular way.

I shall define the I as the self's speaking position. It is the apparent organizer of discrete mental representations from moment to moment. It has great freedom of function: at any time it may link together divergent, even contradictory ideas that derive from previously unrelated streams of thought, and bring them into consciousness, which then leave a trace in memory. Hearing oneself speak, or being heard by others, may lead to a reflective understanding of those links. This is what occurs in free association, as therapist *and* patient hear unconscious thinking.

When immediate transient experiences are voiced, the I also establishes a historical narrative. This does not mean that such enunciated moments are intended to be comments on inner experience; indeed, such an activity would lead to a form of hypertrophied consciousness that would soon shut down unconscious thought. Nonetheless, as parts of the inner world are voiced, generally inaccessible realms of unconscious thought are momentarily projected through the I into speech, and the self becomes both a history maker and the documentarian of this history.

The me refers to the storehouse of the subject's experience of being; the presence of active assumed knowledge. The me is the core self, being registered through experience, transformed into mental axioms that constitute one's mentality or sensibility.

"I" and "me" are not simply parts of speech; they also refer to the linguistic performance of a psychic function. They are employed in internal dialogue between the self and an external other, but they are also part of the assumptions of inner speech, and in that realm divide the self into speaker and listener.

At EBAC, Larry performed for me the distinction between I and me. A day never passed without him walking about the room in rather oddly sensible oscillations, a kind of to-and-fro marked by shifting facial registrations. One day I found him sitting at an abandoned lunch table, moving from one chair to another. The chairs were at the end of the table, one on each side. He would sit in one chair and gesticulate, then quickly switch places to the other chair where he would smile and occasionally laugh.

"Larry, whatever are you doing?"
"I am talking to myself."
"What?"
"Talking to myself."

Part Two

"How are you doing that?"

"When I sit here, I am speaking."

"And when you sit there?" [pointing to the other chair]

"Oh, that's me listening."

"So, who is speaking when you are in the chair you're sitting in now?

"That's for me."

"For you?"

"No, that's for me. That's I speaking, to me, which is in the chair."

"Oh, so when you are speaking, as in saying 'I am going to write a comic book,' then you are saying that to your me that is listening to you, right?"

When Larry walked around the room I realized that this represented a sort of choreography of inner speech. He was engaged in an inner conversation with himself. His oscillations seemed to be spatial enactments of the I talking to the me. For years, I would find myself pondering Larry's enigmatic statements. Had he not shared his secret with me, I am quite sure that I would have failed to grasp the deep significance of the I-me relation that is common in a schizophrenic's inner universe of thought.

Earlier, in Chapter 6, we met my patient Megan, who at first would speak in fragments that made no sense to me. It was some time before I realized that Megan was externalizing inner speech. She was *not* talking to me; she was unknowingly talking to herself in my presence. Much of what she said assumed an awareness of the connecting links between sentence fragments. Because she implicitly assumed her listener was in her mind, and had this awareness and heard her thoughts, she did not have to speak to me.

Assumed Knowledge

If the theories of inner experience explored by authors like Lev Vygotsky and Georges Bataille remain elusive, this is because these phenomena are virtually impossible to describe. Yet writers who address these issues assume we know what they are describing. And if we think about it, many of the core axioms of depth psychology— that we think unconsciously, for example—are similarly predicated on an assumption that we know this from our own inner experience. It would be impossible for anyone to provide scientific evidence of the series of mental events that constitute an emotional inner experience. The laboratory in which these writers work is the inner world— something we all have and know, even if we cannot communicate it.

Rather like Megan, we assume that when we are engaged in talking to ourselves we are having full discussions. In fact, this is an illusion. Although on occasion we may say something simple to ourselves— "Remember to go to the store after work"—our more complicated internal thoughts are not actually enunciated. Unconscious thought processes are extremely complex, occurring in simultaneities of over-lapping and intersecting strands of meaning, subvocally articulated and elaborated. We take these inner discussions for granted, and they operate at the same sort of speed as our dreams.

This assumed knowledge is predicated on the existence of pronom-inal positions (you, me, I, we, they). Verbal grammatical construction is suspended in the lightning-fast process of unconscious thinking, but these positions, part of the assumed, constitute a psychic syntax crucial to unconscious processes of thought. It is assumed that we, as thinkers, are present in our mental productions, that we author them. However, we have very little *conscious* knowledge of what is taking place within the unconscious mind.

It seems that the palimpsest of thought moves forward under the aegis of a mental democracy consisting of speakers and listeners.

Inner speech—the movement of assumed knowledge—must process thoughts deriving from many origins. In that moment-to-moment movement that constitutes unconscious thought, we do not know how much of what we think is from the me—the storehouse of the subject's experience of being—and how much from the I, the presumptuous occupant of the organization of mental representations.

The idea considered in this chapter is that the schizophrenic may have abandoned the conventions of self-other discourse, relinquishing the I so that there is no speaker to re-present the self. Those listening to the schizophrenic are therefore left witnessing the way thought occurs originally, unmediated by what Freud termed "secondary process thinking" or "revision."

However, schizophrenic speech does also include clear units of sensible articulation, so I believe that this schizophrenic action may also reflect something else: an action that I term *psychotic revelation*. This involves the *feeling* that more truths are being expressed in the here-and-now than are uttered by normal conscious verbalization.

Looking at it this way may help us to understand why, certainly in the early stages, many schizophrenics seem to feel that their frightening transformation into psychosis has some silver lining. They are seeing and hearing things the rest of us are oblivious to. Recognizing our apparent obtuseness to their vivid movements of thought—at times crossing optical or auditory fields with incredible speed they give up any hope that they might be understood

For those who are in hospital, matters are not helped by the fact that they also find themselves unable to communicate their thoughts to fellow schizophrenics, who seem as cut off from them as do the normals. Thus many come to believe they are profoundly special, they are the keepers of the truths of the soul, but are destined to an endless isolation.

Assumed Knowledge

As might be evident from my previous descriptions, many of the children at EBAC did not know how to carry on a conversation. Under duress, such as their anxiety about the violence on the streets in Berkeley, they could put many questions to a therapist, but anxiety-driven questioning is clearly not a good conversational idiom.

In my opening chapters I described some of the ways in which the counselors were meant to talk to the children and to engage them, for example by dropping to their knees and looking at them intently, linking vocalization with feeling. By means such as these we would try to enlist them in conversing with us.

Unfortunately, for Ido this never happened, at least not for all the years he was at EBAC. To my knowledge, he never spoke in the first person, and he rarely used the other pronouns that have such a vital role to play in any self's decision about the position they are assuming as they speak.

For other children, either they had not developed the capacity to speak as a subject or, if they had, subjective pronouns (I, you, he, she, it, we, they) were uttered tentatively. They were somewhat more likely to use the objective pronouns (me, you, him, her, it, us, them). And sometimes, even objective pronouns would be avoided. Even though now and then Nick, whom we met earlier, would say "you," he much preferred to address me by my name.

In his sensitive and brilliant essay on Friedrich Hölderlin's descent into schizophrenia, Roman Jacobson quotes Max Eifert's observation of Hölderlin's state of mind as "astray, engaged in an eternal and confusing dialogue with himself." Hölderlin's contemporaries noted that he found it increasingly difficult to talk to people and that his poetry shifted noticeably when he began to engage in a conversation with an internal "you." Famously, he abandoned his own name and adopted a new one—Scardanelli. Jacobson writes: "The disavowal of his own name and the assumption of a loan name or an invented expression is mainly an attempt to eliminate his 'I' from conversations and, later, from his writings as well."[1]

As he withdrew from conversation with others, Hölderlin intensified "a type of partner-directed conversation in spite of the intrasubjective character of such utterances," and he abandoned prose for poetry, which he continued to produce until his death.[2]

Unlike prose, poetry can be composed without any obvious subject or object; indeed, it can be free of pronouns altogether. If we consider, for example, the Chinese language and its poetry, we find a way of speaking the self that does not employ any obvious speaker or addressee. Instead, both language and poetry are highly ambiguous, allowing the reader to project himself into the poem that exists, supposedly, as a transient form of experience.

I am not arguing that the schizophrenic's disappearance from dialogue or his loss of subjective and objective pronouns represents an Eastern way of thinking, but it is fascinating to see how so many schizophrenics abandon the self when they speak, presenting themselves inside an a-syntactical speech world that may have no clear intent at all, although it will leave the listener with powerful impressions. In other words, these communications are almost entirely emotionally based. Often, the schizophrenic is not trying to tell you something; instead, he seeks to wrap you up, syntactically, in his way of experiencing the world.

In his introduction to the poetry of Hölderlin, Michael Hamburger writes, "a lyrical poem is the continuous metaphor of a feeling," while a tragic poem "is the metaphor of an intellectual point of view." As Hölderlin aged and descended into schizophrenia his metaphors of feeling may have become more elusive, but for Hamburger this does not represent a deterioration in his poetry. He suggests that it was as if Hölderlin suddenly became something of a child: "having suffered many rejections and tragedies—he gave up the supposed higher levels of his function, for which he was famous, and spoke from a different place." In Hölderlin's novel *Hyperion*, which, as Hamburger notes, reflects an intensified dualism in his writing and state of mind, the poet writes: "There is an oblivion of all existence, a silencing of all individual being, in which it seems that we have found all things."[3]

Few adult schizophrenics would, in my view, disagree with that statement—certainly not in the early stages of the transformations of their self. If we allow that any self could probably imagine devolving to a point of nearly pure poetic perception, in which the connecting links essential to ordinary discourse are suspended in the interests of another way of seeing the world, then it is not so difficult to grasp the apparent smugness in some schizophrenics who believe they see the world in a superior way. The schizophrenic abandons the I (even used purely as a rhetorical trope) to its dissemination into the world of things, a pantheistic organization in which all selves join in a wordless order, mute yet vivid. He does not know how to tell us where he is, what it is, much less how we could understand this new mental residence.

How do we approach this transformation into a poesis of existence?

The argument thus far has been that our processes of thought are mostly unconscious; we are not therefore in a position to think consciously *about* them. In fact, not knowing that we think unconsciously is vital to our ability to function in the world. In "Everyday Speech," Maurice Blanchot follows the near impossible line of arguing that as all of us live in the everyday, we do so not as organizing subjects but as dumb participants in a movement (the chaos of the everyday) who could not possibly organize the lived into thought. Living in the everyday is the core of our existence, but it has the "trait of being *unperceived.*" It is an area of living that is without significance. It is silent, so silent that it has "already dissipated as soon as we keep still in order to hear it," but we could hear it in "idle chatter," which is a form of silence.[4]

In other words, as we live in the world we may confer meaning upon our experiences, but the everyday, although we experience its presence, is in itself unperceivable and thus outside any possibility of organization into thought.

It is "in the unspeaking speech that is the soft human murmuring in us and around us," writes Blanchot, that "the everyday is movement by which man, as though without knowing it, holds himself back in human anonymity." In the everyday, as participants, we have "no name, little personal reality," and we are "scarcely a figure." He concludes: "The everyday is human."[5]

This anonymity allows us to live in a world that is not determined, in which we are simply parts of something we do not create; indeed, "the everyday is our portion of eternity." It is without direction, has no beginning or end, and is a "storehouse of anarchy."[6]

Living in the everyday, however, is not something the schizophrenic child (and later adult) can do. He cannot forget his authorship and is weighed down by a world that seems constantly to demand from him some form of understanding, enlisting his anxieties, keeping him always on the edge of a precipice over which he might fall into the stream of unconscious thinking.

Blanchot leaves out the question of the function of a self's unconscious in the everyday—perhaps he intends that it be set aside—because unconscious thought is an incessant companion to the minute events taking place in the eternal present. The schizophrenic child does not have a barrier between conscious and unconscious thought; he struggles to find ways of protecting himself from the ideational stream of thoughts derived from the unconscious.

The adult schizophrenic has the benefit of having discovered many defenses against unwanted thoughts and feeling. The sexualization of language is an attempt to control, not simply the primal scene, but the primary process of unconscious thinking and its relation to consciousness.

It is, however, the loss of un-self-conscious participation in the everyday that constitutes the gravest tragedy for the adult schizophrenic. He can no longer simply lose himself in the everyday, free to hear "the unspeaking speech that is the soft human murmuring in us and around us." Those unconscious processes of thought that have woven our own idiomatic pattern through the materials of our world now, for the schizophrenic, punch their way into consciousness—as vivid visual images, powerful bodily dispositions, the sound of accusing voices, or as a smelling of the world, shifting from moment to moment.

Whatever the individual quality of this breach—delusion, vision, hallucination—such patterns are attempts to organize and make sense of the sudden flooding of the self with unconscious thinking that penetrates consciousness. We have no direct experience of unconscious perception except in the dream, and even this is a highly organized sample *from,* but not *of,* the unconscious. Consciousness does not otherwise see its world through unconscious mentation, except now and then in the schizophrenic's world of perception.

If a schizophrenic breakdown is acute, then the person may attempt to make an alliance with this breakthrough and create a sort of private poesis. In this way he will try to contain these outbreaks through poetic expressions (that may seem senseless to others) or through intense "artistic" activities, in which he may rapidly amalgamate unrelated objects as if he is concretizing unconscious thought productions.

Schizophrenic poesis often utilizes the acoustic features of words, infused with a curiously intense rhythmicity that gives body to language. We shall return to this topic when discussing one particular strategy: that of escaping the mind by turning to the body, to body knowledge, and to life recalled from the maternal order.

Impressively, many schizophrenics are able to control their own mental process. Although they may hallucinate, or hide the mind, or return to body knowledge, some may at times be quite lucid and social, apparently restoring themselves to the everyday. Indeed, in those moments one would have to say they were not schizophrenic. Others, however, cannot stem the tide of this breakdown and will resort to outsourcing the mind through projective processes, ultimately seeking to become mindless.

Many schizophrenics have written accounts of their experience of this curious mental state. No two works are even remotely alike, suggesting that human idiom weaves, as always, its distinct pattern through whatever form of so-called personality disorder we suffer.

13

Hiding the Mind

THE EIGHTEENTH-CENTURY village of Stockbridge, Massachusetts, is a fitting location for the gracious buildings that house the
Austen Riggs Center, the last residential treatment provision of its
kind in the United States. The center fits in comfortably with the
brick and clapboard houses on Main Street, and few would know
it was anything other than one of the palatial estates that characterize
the town. It is across the street from the Red Lion Inn, a wonderful
old wood-frame building that dates back to 1773, when it was on
the stagecoach route between Boston and Albany. The inn became
a grand hotel in the mid–nineteenth century, after the Housatonic
Railroad was built and Stockbridge changed from being a sleepy
farming community to a weekend and summer retreat for the
wealthy.

The center was founded in 1919 by Austen Fox Riggs, chartered as
the Stockbridge Institute of Nervous Disorders and Such Other
Charitable Work as may be Incident Thereto. The next year it was
renamed after its founder. To this day its ethos harks back in some
ways to nineteenth-century psychiatry and theories of cure: the idea
that mentally disabled people suffered from a certain character loss

and needed rebuilding through moral reeducation, hard work, and rehabilitation.

My time in London during the mid-1970s working at the PCC and the Tavistock Clinic was followed by nearly ten years spent in the solitude of private practice. Next came the Austen Riggs Center, where I worked in the mid-1980s, and relished the opportunity to be part of a team of fellow clinicians. In addition, I was on the faculty of the Institute of Child Neuropsychiatry of the University of Rome, visiting every other month for a week at a time. This was invaluable, as it returned me to the world of child psychology, and "Via Sabelli" (as it is known to the Romans) was the finest psychiatric hospital for children I have ever known. Over twenty years there I supervised many cases presented by highly gifted clinicians, and life at the hospital was akin to being part of a wonderful family. Frances Tustin and Paula Heimann were the two other regular visitors to this hospital.

At Via Sabelli I continued to work with psychoanalysts and child analysts on the problems posed by the psychotic child. At Riggs, however, I was to learn more about schizophrenics than I could ever have dreamed of.

Schizophrenics create a particular universe, and it is simply not possible for an analyst to enter this idiosyncratic world by working with them in a consulting room. It is essential to see how they create daily life: to get to know where they place certain objects and which parts of a room they avoid and why, to witness various physical movements—their changes of pace and body angle—and where and how they sit.

As we have seen, the person suffering from a catastrophe in his world must find ingenious strategies for survival. I do not mean to deny for a moment, or to romanticize, the immense pain of such a situation, but schizophrenia can be, in its own way, a kind of art form; a vast, complex performance art in which the person moves about in the world, often acting out thoughts rather than speaking them.

Clinicians sometimes speak of patients "killing off" parts of the self or the other, and some personalities—the narcissist, the psychopath—do indeed do this. The schizophrenic, however, will absent himself as a subject in order to hide the self away.

He might, for example, place the aggressive part of the self into a vacuum cleaner, which is suitable partly because of its action (devouring things by sucking them up) and partly because of the angry noise it makes. We might then see him stop by the broom cupboard in the hospital, open the door, cast a glance at the vacuum cleaner and laugh. This action may simply mean, "Hello aggression, glad to see you there, and boy do I know where to find you if I need you! If they only knew . . ."

Similarly, his violent part might be located in a cleaver in the kitchen, where he can visit it now and then in order to be assured that it has not been lost. If the cleaver were to go missing, he could easily become extremely agitated, because he could no longer ascertain the whereabouts of that part of himself. Had it, unbeknownst to him, become lodged somewhere else? Maybe he had murdered someone, in which case the relatives of the victim must be hunting him down. Fleeing to his room, he might hide away until a therapist familiar with his encrypted representational world could reassure him that, even though the cleaver was gone, it was not his fault, nothing had happened, and he was not going to be punished.

We have seen how individual qualities can be placed into people or objects, stored there in order to keep the total personality safe. In more extreme cases the senses themselves become too dangerous to possess and are projected for safekeeping. Seeing, hearing, touching, and smelling become lodged in objects that embody them.

Part Two

I learned about schizophrenic *meandering* one summer's day at Riggs in the building where the patients reside (known as "the Inn"). Ben, a tall, lanky, and almost invisible young man, was walking around the large living room clearly checking on various objects: a book on a shelf, a vase of flowers, a dustbin. He met these objects as if he was simply inspecting their thingness.

At the time I did not give this much thought, but a few days later I saw him repeat the very same actions and then leave the lounge to walk down a long hallway. I followed at some distance. He entered a small room for a few seconds, and then turned left down another hallway that led to some of the patients' bedrooms. I looked into the room and saw there was a table lamp he had switched on. I then caught sight of him ambling out of the Inn and walking toward an area of trees. He stopped at a particular tree, tapped it several times, walked around it, and then went on his way.

A few days later Ben repeated this sequence but with certain differences. This time he turned off the lamp, and when he came to the tree he walked around it in the opposite direction. It was by now clear that his journey was purposeful and logical, although the reasons for his actions were, of course, unknown to me. He had shown me that sometimes schizophrenics think through action. Instead of reflecting on things they *do* things.

Such rituals must be well disguised—one does not want those objects that house his senses to be discovered. In addition, the symbolic objects must be in relatively secure places, preferably remote and unfrequented. In choosing a location for the preservation of one's hearing, for example, it might be considered much safer to project it into a rarely used stethoscope in a nurse's station, say, rather than a radio, which anyone might fiddle around with.

There is a certain genius in how some schizophrenics relate to issues of hearing and listening. Sven, a twenty-seven-year-old farm kid from the Midwest, never seemed to hear what I said to him in our sessions—certainly he would rarely reply to me. I was all the more curious because he seemed bodily studious. He was over six feet tall, slim, with wire-rimmed glasses, bearing the traces of his ancestry— he was of Swedish descent—and being silent was something of a cultural predisposition.

In fact he would defer listening to what was said until he went to his special telephone in a remote part of the Inn. A member of the nursing staff reported that he would pick up the receiver and listen to the dial tone, and then he would "recollect" what had been said in the session. In other words, only once he was at a safe distance could he listen to my words.

This raises an intriguing distinction between the cognitive and the psychic. Cognitively Sven was capable of hearing and listening to me, but psychically he would defer that cognitive possibility until he could take in what I had said through the medium of the telephone. Perhaps he had psychically immunized himself against what actual people said to him in order to give precedence to the voices in his head, so if he was going to hear from me, I myself needed to be reduced to a voice.

In some of the most extreme forms of schizophrenia, the self must hide the mental faculties themselves. The faculty of memory, for example, might be hidden by projecting it into a tape recorder. The person would then be left without any conscious sense of recollection; the tape recorder would be the only object that could perform the act of remembering. Its safety and its reliable functioning would therefore become vitally important.

But what about the moment when a therapist, nurse, or fellow patient refers in conversation to an event in the recent past? At this point we might see the performance of a specific movement, for example, the patient pushing his kneecap with his right index finger.

He is turning on the tape recorder. The machine may not actually be present, but knowledge of its physical existence is sufficiently reassuring to allow him to engage in *symbol borrowing;* the projected faculty's symbolic equivalent is borrowed back in a figurative form. Another possibility is that this mime is not actually performed and the person remains motionless, thinking to himself of the tape recorder. This may serve to reassure him, but if someone happened to mention the tape recorder it would feel alarmingly revealing and cause great anxiety.

Louisa had a habit of snorting in sessions. It was not a form of spontaneous laughter but more a deliberate action, as if she were inhaling the world rather violently. I made a mental note that this seemed to be a form of enraged introjective identification: she needed to take something in but it was an irritating thing to have to do. Her snorting was all the more apt, as Louisa was one of the first mixed martial arts "fighters" in her neck of the woods (Oregon), and her appearance—she was short, very stocky, and cultivated a small beard—added to her somewhat fearsome presence.

As time passed, she revealed a particular interest in vacuum cleaners. She did not like the one at the Inn because it did not seem powerful enough, but nonetheless she would visit it every so often in its storage locker. One day she let me know that vacuum cleaners were important because they cleansed the atmosphere of dangerous toxins. I said I noticed that she snorted in sessions, and wondered if she was inhaling materials in the room to cleanse the environment and make the world safer for herself. Louisa gave me a grin, as if to say, "Okay, you figured this out."

Our elucidation of this did not eliminate the snorting, nor did it remove her interest in the vacuum cleaner, but it did significantly diminish her need to check on it. She proceeded to tell me all the sorts of things in the object world that she did not like: ideas, people, entire localities, and so forth. Having seen her mother vacuuming the house as a child, she associated its actions with anger and with the elimination of the unwanted. Once we could comprehend its meaning, her use of this object made perfect sense.

However, my understanding of this produced a new set of problems. When she grasped that I could see the meaning of her snorting, she asked me if we had just had intercourse. I asked what she meant. She said she thought I must have had intercourse with her because I had gotten into her, and maybe we should be reporting this. I said that what she was saying was very important: it seemed to me that she had found my discovery a bit exciting and this had led to her wondering whether intercourse had taken place. Louisa agreed that she had felt excited, and she then spoke in surprisingly frank terms about why she avoided people: she found being understood disturbing because it was arousing.

A lot has been said in psychological texts about "concrete thinking." It is easy enough to appreciate what is meant by this phrase. A therapist reported that he once said to a patient, "You can't have your cake and eat it," to which the patient replied: "Cake, what cake? I don't want any cake!" This was cited as an example of a failure to appreciate the metaphoric nature of language and was seen as a typical psychotic concretization of the symbolic.

The problem with this generalization, however, is that, even though they may do it in a concrete way, schizophrenics *do* symbolize. Indeed, one might say that they live in a world that is overwhelmed by the arbitrary nature of their symbolic order. The name of an object, such as "tape recorder," is equivalent to the object. To speak these words is, in effect, to tamper with the patient's actual tape recorder: word and thing are equivalent. This is a form of symbolization, one that Hanna Segal termed "symbolic equation."[1] The word stands for the thing, the thing stands for a function of the personality, hence the word stands for the personality function. To use the name of the object is therefore very nearly the same as physically handling it. It is close enough for the schizophrenic to yell "No tape recorder!" meaning, "Do not talk about the tape recorder!" Or he might say nothing, but put his hands over his ears and rock silently back and forth. This involves the language of the physical in a form of object elimination, a reversal achieved by symbolizing the act of not hearing. By rocking back and forth, his body and mind unite in a symbolic act of anal elimination: the sound of the words "tape recorder" are evacuated.

Schizophrenic reversibility is the two-way street of schizophrenic symbolization. The tape recorder is memory. The self puts it there. But happening upon the tape recorder then means that the self is now suddenly confronted by the presence of memory. Multiply this reversibility many times—including the projection of aspects of the object world, parts of the self, the senses, functions of the mind—and one can appreciate how easily the schizophrenic can feel invaded.

What if this invasiveness is unbearable?

It is not difficult to understand how the function of memory can be placed in a tape recorder. It is an object that records past conversations. But precisely because of its accuracy it is perhaps too transparent, and the person might need to choose a less discernible object via a more complex chain of associations. So memory might be projected into something not obviously related, such as, for example, the Missouri River. How might the Missouri River embody memory? We could say that it offers the notion of "the river of time," and it also has a historic place in the American past. In an East Coast hospital it is far enough away that there might not be a need to worry about anyone tampering with it, and it is unlikely to come up in conversation. Further, its secrecy would be easy to preserve—a therapist would have to work very hard to discover this projection.

Let us think now about some aspects of the projective process.

The tape recorder is a physical object, close both in space and in function to the idea of memory. The Missouri River is a physical object distant in space and also in symbolic function. The tape recorder is a *close projection*, while the river is a *distant projection*.

Bion wrote about "bizarre objects," and I want to borrow from his concept as we think of forms of projection that are, for all intents and purposes, undiscoverable. Imagine that memory is projected into an abstract, nonphysical object, such as a random sequence of numbers: 0365. This sequence can be imbued with a kind of magical presence by incantation, as the person repeats it many times a day. The chanting may even be silent and internal, so that the digital sequence is never actually uttered. This "object" will be almost impossible to discover. The schizophrenic has hidden his memory where it cannot be found.

In assessing the degree of seriousness of schizophrenia, one can differentiate in terms of types of projection: some will be close (the tape recorder), some distant (the Missouri River), and some will be bizarre (the number sequence). Close projection is relatively discoverable. It is most common for schizophrenics to project themselves at first into objects of this kind. The longer a person inhabits the schizophrenic order, the more likely it is that the projections will become distant. The bizarre, abstract form is most typical of the most unreachable schizophrenics, those who are termed "catatonic" or "vegetative."

We can also differentiate degrees of schizophrenia based on what is projected, how systematically, and how completely. If the schizophrenic projects his sexual states of mind into a range of objects that allow one to discover the sexual dynamic, then it is clear that this person is reachable and has a wish to be found. So if he talks about Britney Spears, then about rabbits chasing one another on the lawn, and then about kangaroos, we can easily track his free associations as he imagines a sexual object (intercourse), and then birth and mothering.

Mental contents are more easily discernible than the projection of mental processes. As in the example above, contents usually appear as a series of related ideas, forming a pattern that unconsciously reveals what is being thought about. But when a mental process is projected, the contents go with it and the agency of the mind will often evade discovery.

Let us think, for example, about what might happen to the sexual feelings of the schizophrenic. We must distinguish here between metasexuality and sexuality proper. The former is not experientially sexual—it is agitating and anxiety-provoking—and the latter is an expression of the schizophrenic's own independent sexual life. The question is, what is done with it?

Rather than thinking of sexual contents, let us consider what happens to the mental process that thinks sexually. In normality this might involve perceiving and thinking about sexual beings present in the room (maybe staff members or other patients), also masturbatory fantasies and memories of moments when the self was attracted to another person. The schizophrenic, however, is unlikely to mention any sexual topic; indeed, he may appear to be sexually oblivious.

To empty the self of a mental process is a very radical action. In the example to follow, there is a complete and systematic elimination of sexuality from the self's world. The part of the mind that processes sexuality is placed in a physical object that now stands both for process and contents.

Tom has lodged the sexual part of his mind in cooking. A meal becomes a sexual object; food preparation represents foreplay or masturbation. When a dish is placed in the oven this stands for intercourse, the cooking process for pregnancy, and the arrival of the meal for birth. Cooking is a process of transformation. So sexuality-the-process has been displaced onto cooking-the-process.

If Tom should become sexually aroused in the presence of another, he might refer (or transfer) this to the kitchen index, placing his sexual arousal into an object: "You are putting a bun in my mouth, aren't you?" We can see here that by mixing the index he arranges for an idiosyncratic combination. (The usual expression is "a bun in the oven," but here it is transposed to "a bun in my mouth.") Or he might say something like, "a burner is in my match," referring to objects that can be found in the kitchen. Having housed the self's sexual arousal inside the language of a specific container, he is free to combine the objects in any way he wishes.

He does not need to hang out in the kitchen to guarantee this transfer. In fact he might avoid spending time there and hardly ever allude to the lexicon of this index. "Out of sight, out of mind" is the schizophrenic strategy. The object needs to be somewhere between the human and the non-human worlds, far enough away that it cannot obviously be connected to him.

If he does find himself in the kitchen, or maybe even when eating food, Tom may become highly anxious. Since the cooking process is equivalent to the sexual process, what he is doing when he is eating becomes highly complex. What is cooked is the result of a form of intercourse. How is he to cope with this?

The most common defense is what I call the *schizophrenic fetish*. This is any object, or action, that the schizophrenic views as essential to his participation in an event or in transactions with others. For example, Tom may dispossess the meal of its sexuality by spitting on it. It might be safe to eat only the potatoes. Or he may pass his face close to the meal, humming to himself. The action transforms the event. By doing something to the food in this way he reconsecrates it. It is now momentarily redefined.

Metasexuality, even if it is agitating and provokes anxiety, may be enlisted to banish contact with the schizophrenic's actual, physical sexual life. The *idea* that he controls all forms of intercourse satisfies him that he is being sexual (even if this is not so) and his own particular sexuality is subordinated within a metasexual organization.

As we have seen, schizophrenics are adept at hiding away their mental processes. Sven, a severely ill patient, whose ritual process we discussed above, was terrified that he was in danger from what he saw (in reality, in dreams, or in hallucinations), so he went undercover and projected this perceptual apparatus into a lamp in a room that was seldom used. When distressed by something seen, he would walk into the room, switch on the lamp, and leave. The lamp was meant to contain and to perform the process of seeing. If he had a thought that was too much for him (he mentally "saw" something), he blamed the lamp for failing to protect him. He might turn it off or unplug it. He might smash it to bits.

Over a short period of time many such mental processes may be housed in objects that perform them. This is a more dynamic situation than the housing of specific contents—the mother, the sibling, the father—who may also be allocated to objects around the institution in which the schizophrenic finds himself. When he first arrives in a hospital he will quickly invest objects with parts of the mind and mental contents. If he is living alone, or at home with his parents, he may maintain an even greater degree of control over his projected objects, and this allows him to live in a highly solipsistic universe. One of the reasons that schizophrenics resist going to hospital is that they will lose their known projective universe, the world that contains their history and parts of their mind.

Hiding the Mind

But even this degree of control does not keep him safe. The fact is that projective identification works only up to a point. And a mind projected is a mind lost; what is left cannot possibly deal with the vicissitudes of life.

When an object no longer succeeds in containing a particular mental process or content, this failure feels to the person like a failure of *object constancy*. This is compounded by *schizophrenic emptiness*, the subjective state that results from projecting the self into the object world. The aim—to rid the self of its mind—succeeds to some extent, but it leaves the person feeling hollow. Some schizophrenics say they feel light as a feather, that the wind might blow them away if they go outside. Others walk as if they are a-gravitational, almost seeming to glide a few inches above the ground. Some can inhabit a room without other patients being aware of their presence.

Beset by mental contents and a mind that can no longer be trusted to think the self's thoughts, the projection into objects becomes a prolonged process of *psychic disinhabitation*. Devices such as the radio and television are used to assist in this—in fact those who live with their parents will often spend most of their time watching TV. By tuning in to the same programs on the same channels every day of the week, they can give themselves over to a TV mind, which is both a mental process and a container of mental contents. To turn it on is to turn on the alternative to having a mind, to find a substitute for one's own mental contents.

Although some aspects of this are quite ordinary, it is incorrect to assume that schizophrenics are watching TV in the way non-psychotic people do. They are not "taking in" characters, plots, or events. Making an appointment with the right program, which contains the familiar characters and plot atmospheres, they can use the regular characters and storylines to house the self. The TV becomes a kind of mental vacuum cleaner sucking out the remaining mental contents that still inhabit the self.

It will come as no surprise, then, that there might be a preference for sitcoms and cartoons over news and documentaries, or that there may be panic and a violent reaction if another patient changes the channel. This is not an average irritation at the interruption of a favorite program, but is instead a threat to a kind of life support unit and a feeling of being suddenly endangered.

Psychic disinhabitation is a form of identification with the aggressor, although in a most ironic way. In a psychotic twist of logic, one who empties *himself* into the environment develops, over time, a belief that something or somebody has robbed him of himself. In some this may remain merely a background thought, but in paranoid forms of such thinking it can lead to violent action against others who are assumed to have something that was once their own possession.

The concept of the death drive is useful in thinking about how withdrawal of emotional investment from the object world forms a psychotic enclave aimed at a reversal of interest in the world. By withdrawing from the imaginary and symbolic orders and converting human elements into *things*, the schizophrenic creates a ghost town. Although from time to time he is reanimated—a smile crosses his face, a memory occurs to him, there is a brief moment of contact with another—he will return to the *schizophrenic gaze* that stares into middle distance. This is a place where there is, seemingly, nothing to look at, but precisely because it is a nothing-space it becomes the place of negative hallucinations. To use James Grotstein's concept of the black hole, middle distance is the location of anti-matter in which objects are destroyed. So to stare into it is to be in a place where experience in real time is eradicated as it happens.[2]

The schizophrenic often seems to become preoccupied with parts of his body or bits of lint on his clothing, as if he is suddenly in a state of absorption. I term this *schizophrenic business*. It is a defense against human encounter and the anticipated demands of conversation should the other arrive.

If he does become engaged in conversation, he will often try to negotiate a *schizophrenic contract* in which it is agreed that there are definite "no-go areas" of conversation or action. This contract can be complex and multifaceted. Let us imagine that he has projected a part of himself into the concept "island." An embargo will then apply not only to the word "island," but also to all the clusters of associations surrounding that word—"Bali," a traffic island in the road, Ireland, the phrase "I land," and so forth. A mention of any of these linked words will amount to invasion of the true self and may lead to immediate agitation.

If he had chosen a wardrobe to contain an aggressive part of himself, the place for putting coats might become the area for the burial of murdered objects. So if one were to say, "Let me put your coat in the wardrobe," it could raise intense anxiety: the dead will arise to haunt him.

Often there may be a whole range of physical objects, images, gestures, and words that carry projected parts of the schizophrenic's mind, or specific mental contents. He may indicate the "no-go areas" in various ways, and not necessarily verbally. Once I used a certain word to describe something, and the patient immediately panicked and plugged his ears. I was aware I had done something very alarming. I had inadvertently used a word that was a projection, and this had felt like an attack. I told him that I had obviously said something that was too shocking, we ascertained which word it was, and I assured him that I would not use this word again in his presence.

One becomes aware of a kind of psychotic minefield in which both words and things may be dangerous, and over time one develops a kind of mariner's chart of how to navigate in the individual's world in order to avoid these dangerous objects. Unless one respects this defensive structure to begin with, I do not think it is possible to earn the patient's trust. But when he realizes that the analyst understands that he experiences certain things as terrifying, and that the other will not impose his will on those objects, he may feel increasingly safe.

Many of the mechanisms we have been discussing are designed to protect the schizophrenic against *psychotic empathy*. Because of his skill in projecting himself into objects, of hiding his mind, he is at risk when it comes to relationships with other people. If the other for whom they feel affection comes to harm, either through a breakdown or by suffering some physical injury, the schizophrenic can have become so identified with the person that this becomes his own suffering. Any attempt to interpret his projections can lead him to believe that the clinician is trying to remove him from himself, and this can create extreme alarm. At the same time, the inability to cure the other of the state they are in, and the fact that he is fated by identification to *be* the other, ties him to an indeterminate vector that mirrors his own history of being fated by external factors.

14

Dodging Thought

AS DISCUSSED, IN THE EARLY STAGES of a breakdown the schizophrenic self starts to project the I, often into elements of the natural surroundings. It speaks through these objects and the self follows the directives of the voice. We have understood this as a way of trying to remain in secret contact with the I.

After a while, however, this proves to be exhausting. Try as the self might to follow the vocal directives, these can become increasingly unrealistic, and the tone of the voice can shift from a seemingly friendly presence to something harsh and threatening. As more time passes, the voices may no longer be linked to objects in the outside world but take up habitation inside the self. (For many, this will have happened from the beginning.) They will still be heard as foreign to the self, and may continue to have a human dimension, but as the years go by their messages turn increasingly into abstract, disembodied auditory directives.

One's natural aim is to preserve the mind against annihilation, and at first a schizophrenic may employ the tactic of befriending the voices—"if you can't beat them, join them." But when this fails, then what?

Having projected the I into vocal substitutes—thus dislodging its centrality in the mind as the self's speaker—it may now return as the voice of God, or some other powerful abstract authority. This tends to happen when the self is deteriorating further and senses the danger of annihilation; the power of the external voice is in inverse proportion to the degree of self-authorship. Following the voice of God, then, is an indexical measure of the need for guidance at a time of considerable threat to the self.

Since the mind has been outsourced through projections, there is very little the self can do to process passing thoughts expressed by the voices. A common means of dealing with this dilemma is to prevent a thought from occurring by taking action. These actions must by definition be senseless, as their purpose is to defy reason (thinking). To think is to open the door to deeply disturbing images, ideas, and directives. It is at this stage that the person may "hit the road" and wander, often undressing or taking off his shoes and living outdoors for days at a time. Initially this might be part of "running with nature," a defense that objectifies a fear of people and the social order, but eventually it becomes a means of doing things that seem to make no sense at all.

Friends, family members, and therapists are likely to find themselves bewildered by this behavior. A person may urinate in public, stand naked in a public square, hide under a bridge, or walk into a mud flat and become stranded. These actions are both senseless and sense-full. The body seems to take the place of the mind as the self moves into the world naked, exposed to the elements, in a kind of body-to-body encounter with the real. By being senseless in the world of thought but sense-full in the realm of bodily experiences, the person reverses the impact of mind upon the self by substituting body and action for thinking.

A friend may say, "What he is doing just doesn't make sense." And that is the point. By allowing an impulse action to occur at the moment when the self senses the onset of a thought, action defeats thinking.[1]

Becoming increasingly mindless, the person reverses his position of being a victim. He is now in charge of making nonsense, thereby assuming a certain control over his own fate and his relation to others. He is on the run, and will initially be deeply afraid of being put back into hospital, as this would force him out of his created, physical world and back into the realms of thought, where he will once again become the target for any passing mad idea.

As he becomes increasingly mindless, he may eventually succeed in defeating the efforts of family, friends, and therapists to make sense of his actions. And that is his aim. Ironically, at this point people give up trying to make any sense of the schizophrenic and resort to actions: "I just can't take it anymore, I am going to have to hospitalize him."

Those who are involved with him stop posing questions and searching for meaning, and over time they begin to protect themselves from thinking about him. As he resists the actions they are taking, this irony may not escape their attention: they themselves are increasingly behaving as he does. He may find comfort in defeating others' ability to think; as he no longer has his own mind, entrusting mental contents to anybody else's feels intrinsically hazardous.

Senselessness is common after a breakdown, but looking back on their lives with this person, friends and family may recall times in the past when he did odd things, things that did not make sense. These were, and can later be recognized as, precursory moments when the individual sensed the onset of disturbing ideas and abreacted them by doing something strange.

Vince, for example, had developed a strategy of rapidly moving his hands to create odd, abstract shapes, often at school or in public places. On occasion his actions caused amusement, but most times people found them perplexing and distressing. Unconsciously he was passing the thought process from himself to others. They were fated to try to figure out what he was meaning, and when he saw defeat in the eyes of the other he would be relieved. He had proactively prevented an emerging thought from crossing his own mind by engaging in impulsive action.

Such preventive measures do not necessarily involve physical movements. Earlier, I described how my patient Megan lay mostly silent on the couch for the first months of her analysis. Her need to be left alone in my presence was palpable. I felt I was in touch with her but neither of us said a thing.

When she finally began to speak coherently, what she reported was very disturbing and yet rather precise.

Megan had not run naked in the streets or defecated on the floor of a public lavatory. Instead she had defied language. For a long time she was the embodiment of the alternative to sense-making.

By connecting the self to things, by thinging the self into an it rather than an I, by abandoning the symbolic order, the schizophrenic tries to evade the perils of thought and language. Even when speaking, he will do so as it were under license—a few moments in which he communicates from within the ironic realm of an illusion. The self speaks as an I but undermines semantic sensibility in favor of syntactical agglomerations. No-thing thinks. And if the self is to be disinhibited in the interests of survival, if it is being hunted down by thoughts on the loose, if it is to defeat the mind and yet remain somehow viable, then it has to play a game. So speech is utilized and an illusion of sense is created.

At Riggs, one patient would sometimes enter a session and put an object on the desk next to his chair: a rock, a mushroom, a book. He would place it with a sort of studied indifference that would, of course, draw attention to it. If asked about it he would say something like "it is a rock" or "this is a mushroom," as if to humor the therapist, mocking any attempt to understand him. Things-in-themselves have no meaning, a state he intended for himself. I on the other hand was a person invested with the task of discovering what my patient meant by his actions, his statements and his way of being.

Defeating efforts to think with and about him was crucial to his need for meeting thing-to-thing. The therapist had to be diminished to a point where I understood nothing and where all we shared was an insensible affinity. We were to be reduced from linguistic creatures to selves with only nonverbal forms of communion. These elements of relating were of great interest to psychoanalysts such as Winnicott, Khan, John Klauber, and Nina Coltart, for whom silence bore core truths, as a form of communication that existed before the wording of the self.

It will be clear from the preceding discussion that it would be incorrect to interpret all schizophrenic actions as senseless—sometimes there is a discernible underlying logic to what the person is instructed to do. But often the voices will be sending him on meaningless journeys, albeit with majestic assurance that such actions are fulfilling some divine purpose. So the voices are a compromise formation, between thoughts that could cross the mind and disturb the self, and vocalized ideas that are statements with no meaning except as auditory transitional phenomena urging imminent activity. To obey what the voice says is to undo the voice as a thought or idea and transfer it into action.

The person aims to defeat the terrifying hallucinations or shocking vocal directives by embodying an action figure that follows instructions. It is an odd paradox. At the very moment when he is cut off from the I that might position representations of unconscious thoughts into consciousness, he feels that thought, being, and action are bundling up into an extraordinary intimacy. Rarely have mind, body, existence, and reality felt so intimately connected.

I have discussed how, in childhood or adolescence, some schizophrenics may already have been managing to hide their madness within seemingly conventional eccentric behavior; they know eccentricity is somehow accepted and that they will be able to get away with this performance. They sense that something is happening; premonitions, perhaps, of what is to come. Then comes what those around them might term a breakdown and what some schizophrenics often describe as a conversion or a religious experience, and their previous existence is relegated to another realm.

While friends and family are becoming anxious, the schizophrenic is dealing with very dire matters indeed. The world shifts according to hallucinogenic interventions. The self is divested of much of its historical agency as voices start to tell it what to do. Although a sense of self continues, the person feels besieged, and has to survive inside a new and challenging set of circumstances.

From the beginning the schizophrenic will usually develop some form of explanation for what has happened. After a while, if the self is not restored to its history—the "ordinary" place in the self's narrative from which is generated a sense of the present and visions of the future—he will opt for the construction of a parallel universe.

I see this as rather ingenious.

Caught in a world of hallucinatory visions and voices, thrown into an unknown reality, with scant choice, forced to concede he has been morphed into a different world, he struggles to form some sense of it all. He may seek a focus for this world, an object that often becomes a fount of wisdom and intuitive judgment. Wandering the landscape, he might find an ancient oak tree and invest it with divine power. He may choose it for its majestic physical presence which magically generates all kinds of derivative meaning. When he then sees the letter "O" on a placard outside a store selling telephones, this may be a manifestation of the oak tree, as it mirrors the sound of "oak." Or he may hear the sound in discussions taking place around him: "Oh, I'm not so sure about that"; "I'll see you later . . . oh, wait, I'm busy tonight." The tree spreads its branches far and wide.

Secret affiliations are formed between the self's sensorial being (as one who sees, hears, smells, and feels), the physicality of the object world (the oak tree), and private signifiers deriving from that link: the sound "O." Such derivatives start to appear everywhere as if the unconscious now permeates consciousness. The self adheres to this form of intelligence inhabiting a different world, a parallel reality that seems more densely interconnected, more imbued with meaning, than one's prior life in the humdrum.

While mothers, fathers, siblings, and friends bear the loss of this former self, the person may believe he has discovered a new universe not seen by others. Trees, streams, wind, sheep, rocks—objects in the world—are talking and the schizophrenic can hear them and be guided by them. Like with any human experience, people vary in the way they respond to their schizophrenia. Some seem rather intoxicated by the objects speaking to them; others may be terrified of their transportation into a new order of things.

It is an interesting feature of this parallel existence that there seems to be some degree of choice about which voice to follow and which to decline. One of the patients at Riggs, Sam, let me in on aspects of his alternative universe. It was clear that he did not see himself as a mindless subject within it. He could be amused by certain visual and auditory hallucinations, as if exercising some kind of discerning judgment. No doubt he was living elsewhere and thought I was missing out.

Was he massaging his dilemma? Was he trying, like some appa-ratchik, to apologize for an oppressive regime? It did not seem so. It was more akin to a religious conversion experience in which he felt he had experienced a stunning vision and needed me to know it.

Sam was not a mindless convert. He seemed at times to be star-tlingly in touch, quite sane and lucid—almost the person of old. These were refreshing moments, though quite disturbing in their own right. Further, his attempts to stop his thought processes hardly seemed to endorse his apparently enthusiastic embracing of his brave new world. If it was so wonderful, why not go with it?

Well, in some ways many did. Indeed, as if being schizophrenic were not enough, some are able to embellish their experience with all sorts of hallucinogens. But these efforts overdose the psychotic dimension, trying to comatose the self. The schizophrenic has to tread a fine line, maintaining both a surreptitious connection to sanity and the outside world, and an apparently intimate relation to his new hal-lucinogenic reality.

For some schizophrenics it feels imperative to conceal their situation, and hospital can (ironically) seem like a good solution. This is not only because they are physically safe there, but because the staff are generally so overworked that they have no time to talk to them. So they are left alone. There is no one seeking to stir up thoughts, no one to disturb inner conversations with the many voices populating the mind. A weekly meeting with a psychiatrist is simply a ceremonial occasion in which reality and medications are reviewed. Other patients may break the custodial order, but if you wish to get out to return to madness then you must encourage the staff to feel they have done a good job. So adept schizophrenics learn how to emulate sanity, and often these dramatic portrayals are amusing to other patients and the staff.

Dodging Thought

147

15

Somatoforms

ERNST HAD REMOVED HIMSELF from his family in a systematic manner. He would not speak to them or eat with them, and he performed only the most essential tasks. A petite and pale young man with light blond hair, Ernst could be in a room and remain almost unnoticed. He blended in with the non-human environment as if he were a part of the room's furnishing. Indeed, eventually he would tell me with some gratification about events he attended when people afterward said to him, "You were there?"

He was the youngest of four children and often pointed out that he physically lived in the shadows of two older brothers who were quite tall and hefty.

In his sessions with me he described his psychotic convictions in great detail. He celebrated his disappearance from the human world, and for some weeks he practiced the act of removing mental contents from his mind so that it would be utterly empty. He would help himself do this by not eating or drinking for days on end, by entering a period of intense hallucination (which he did not enjoy), followed by a trance-like state in which he could sit for an entire day without moving. He felt he was in a state of peace and that this was where he wished to live.

He started to realize, however, that what he thought he had under control—making objects disappear or change shape—was less and less within his grasp. Things began to appear, morph, or vanish without him being in charge.

In addition, although he had developed a private language, one that others found incomprehensible, he also found it harder and harder to speak. It was as if the words he intended to articulate no longer showed up.

The shifting nature of his perceptions and his alarming loss of vocalization resulted in a dramatic shift in his body state. He now moved in visibly stiff ways, perspired profusely, and began to laugh in a way that sounded like a bark.

Months passed before I realized that Ernst's language was somewhat like Megan's, the mumbling of inner speech. He was literally "speaking out loud," but not in articulate units of speech. His thoughts were simply being released into vocalization, which had gone on for such a long time that he had retrospectively conferred upon his articulations the notion that he had developed a private language.

When I realized this I said, "You do know that I cannot understand what you are saying"—he nodded—"but I realize, Ernst, it is because you are mumbling." I then told him I was not in his mind and could not listen to his thought processes. Would he be kind enough to slow down and articulate those thoughts in speech?

It was as if I was the first person to ever say this to him. In fact, many people had noticed Ernst's way of speaking, but apparently no one felt inclined to tell him. How had he managed to get along for so many years doing this, I wondered? It turned out that, in fact, he was articulate until about two years before he began analysis with me. It was only then that he began to speak differently, and it was one of the reasons he was referred for help.

Over the next years Ernst reported not so much what was on his mind but what he tried to do with his mind. Our work was often a kind of philosophical consideration of the benefits (or in his view, deficits) of having a mind to think thoughts. Gradually, he came to accept his mind and to report thoughts that crossed it. His emerging schizophrenia had been encountered, and after five years of analysis five times a week, we stopped our work.

Years later, Ernst resumed analysis.

He was curious about why he had developed such an acute sensitivity to cloth—clothing or otherwise—that verged on an allergy. He had to launder his clothing in a special soap, he could not bear to come into contact with other people's garments, he could only sleep in his own bed sheets, and was sleepless when he stayed in hotels and so forth.

Ernst's allergies were not new.

When his parents bought him a new bed when he was fourteen, he developed an allergy—maybe to the filling in the mattress . . . or maybe to the sheets . . . or the pillows. From that point forward each object was intently examined, but nothing seemed to explain his reaction. Significantly, it was never properly somatic—he did not break out into a rash—but his anxiety escalated to the point of such extreme agitation that his doctor recommended a rest. The new bed was replaced, first with his old bed, then with no bed at all, and finally he slept on a yoga mat.

Ernst's allergies were familiar. Anything new was a potential psychic toxin, but he would also suddenly announce, out of the blue, that he found some household object that had been around for years—a lamp, a newspaper rack, a kitchen chair—uncomfortable and disturbing. He would demand that others regard his somatic experience as irreducible, and when his family tried to help—"Why don't you just give it time and see how it goes?"—this would merely lead to further agitation.

He was disturbed by the sensation of touch but also by changes in light, sound, and smell. If a guest inadvertently left an overhead light on in the hallway when he was seated at the dining-room table he would become increasingly disquieted. Eventually his mother or father would say, "Ernst, is something bothering you?" He would reply, "The light from the lamp is bothering me," and someone would get up and turn it off.

If he heard neighbors speaking in the adjoining flat, or a lorry moving up the street, or the rattle of dustbins, or the creak of footsteps on the floor at night, he would develop a somatic hurt: he would *feel* this as an assault on his soma.

He segregated and outlawed specific foods—no jam, no hard cheese, no broccoli—as well as certain methods of cooking: nothing baked in an oven. He was extremely taste sensitive, and if, for example, any crushed almond or coconut milk had found its way into a meal his response was immediate and sometimes almost violent.

Every day of his life Ernst found the world irritating.

We had so many other issues to confront during his first analysis that these allergies were not overlooked but simply did not compete with the more psychotic manifestations of his thinking. And toward the end of the analysis they disappeared, so it seemed irrelevant to pursue their meaning.

In the second analysis, he asked if he had ever told me about the person who raised him. I thought he meant his mother, but he corrected me: no, he meant his nanny who had looked after him until he was ten. I had not heard of this before.

It seemed that he had become the sole object of the nanny's life. She would be heavily perfumed, often touching or embracing him, talking to him, gazing into his eyes, and so forth. In fact she was not just a nanny, she was his aunt—his mother's sister. Mother and aunt were twins and they shared a similar idiom: both were extremely intense, and this left Ernst constantly agitated.

Even though we shall never know what infants think, we can assume that their first experiences of the world are sensory. These will be made up in utero, for example, of the sound of the mother's heart and internal organs, the infiltration of light, the senses of movement and taste, and later the sense of smell. What is important is the heterogeneity of the primitive sensorium in its apprehension of lived experience.

I believe that many schizophrenics return to this early sensorial world, to *somatoform experience and representation*. Before wording or conceptual thinking, somatoforms express the self's nascent experience through the body's lexicon.

One difficulty we face in understanding schizophrenics is the extent to which we have lost touch with such early forms of experience and representation.

We react to our experience of the object world in many different ways. As an infant, if we taste something that we do not like, we spit it out. As an adult, we tend to screw up our faces and push the food away. Any structured (that is, predictable) form of sensorial expression is a somatoform.

If Ernst heard something he did not like the sound of, he would bend his head to the left, hunch over, and cover his ears. If he tasted a food he did not like he would spit it out onto his hand and put it back on the plate. If he smelled an unpleasant odor he would hold his nose or leave the room. If he felt a texture that he found irritating he would recoil. Over the years those who knew him became sensitive to these evolved and differentiated somatoform representations, and they knew how powerful his reactions could be.

What people take to be signs of paranoia in a schizophrenic—the fact that he thinks he knows what others are feeling or thinking by reading the expressions on their faces or their body language—may in fact simply be an indication that he is reading their somatoforms. Those of us who have passed beyond this stage to the linguistic level of representation generally pay much less attention to this earlier form of expression, although of course we are not oblivious to it; indeed, in love relations and other intimate forms of personal encounter, we often return to the language of the body. Mothers, for example, are compelled by the nature of their infant's somatic knowing to return to sensorial life. Some mothers and fathers, compromised perhaps by the complexity of their adult lives, may be less than skillful in this area. This does not make them bad parents, but it may mean they are less easily able to translate and thus transform the sensorial, the baby's somatoform expression, into forms of verbal expression.

Coexistent with sensorial experience and somatoformation is the infant's affective response to those experiences. The two most fundamental negative affects at this point in life are anxiety and anger, with depression a close third. In a good-enough situation when sensorial experience leads to a clear somatoform—such as feet-kicking, crying, et cetera—the caretaker may *sense* the root of the infant's affective state. The mother will often intuitively know that, for example, the baby is expressing anxiety about being left alone as opposed to skin irritation, hunger, or any other possible somatic stimulus. The problem is therefore solved through an integration of mutual sensorial experiencing, attuned affective expressions, and verbal utterances.

A fascinating challenge of working with the schizophrenic is that he may have reverted almost entirely to sensorial life and to somatoform representation. Ernst was a good teacher in this respect.

He returned to analysis because some of these phobic symptoms had reemerged, and he now wanted to understand them. He was also decidedly curious about what had taken place years before, and he now wanted a deeper, reflective understanding of his schizophrenia. (He was very frank about his diagnosis and used the term in nondefensive ways.)

I would listen to his reflections, very deeply rapt by his determination to explain schizophrenia to me. He needed, now, to understand his sensorial grasp of life and how and in what ways it had impeded his development. He was also troubled by his ways of thinking at times, which he argued "seem on the verge of madness."

He told me that as he walked the streets on occasion his thought world troubled him. He had visited Rome, and while rounding the corner to the Pantheon he was struck by his anger over a stranger passing too close to him. On another walk near the Tiber he found another complete stranger equally infuriating. Sitting on the side of a fountain in the Piazza Navonna, he was again overcome with irritation by a person who sat within a few feet of him.

Sessions were taken up with rather meticulous descriptions of these outings. Then he told me of a recent flight to Moscow. He described a complex emotional experience that involved feeling generally anxious, then angry, then becoming specifically irritated by a fellow passenger. After more than two hours of bearing this person pushing his seat back and forth and putting his hands behind him on the head rest, Ernst said, "Would you *please* be still!"

He was horrified. I congratulated him. I said he had managed to move from sensorial distress and affective disturbance into speech. I asked whether he had felt relieved by this. He said he had, but that he expected he had gone mad. I said I thought he had gone sane for a moment, and we laughed.

The next months of work concentrated on the ever present "pool of anxiety and anger" in him, and he told me with great shame that he thought he only left his flat in order to get rid of this. He would glare at someone, or make what he believed was a visible bodily gesture toward them that communicated his anger. These were all somatoform expressions; his feelings were never verbalized.

For many years Ernst had hidden within a world meant to be apprehended and defined only according to the senses. He attempted to rid himself of those sense experiences (for example, the experience of being with other people) that displeased him, and aimed for a disincarnated metaphysical universe split off from all reality, both bodily and environmental.

He could bear to be in a room, or eat a meal, or spend time with other people only as long as he could find some way to get the group to discuss an arcane theological-philosophical issue. He was highly educated, and this often worked. His companions would say, "So Ernst, what interesting ideas have crossed your mind?" and he would spout something forth. He found that by far the best ploy was to enunciate with gravity an almost nonsensical statement that was intended to arouse avid interest. The sole purpose of these expositions was to disincarnate himself and the group, in order to inhabit a realm devoid of sense.

This tactic would not, of course, work for an entire evening. For some years Ernst would end up drinking himself into oblivion, or simply zone out and daydream. In this state, thoughts would manifest in the sort of abstract form that might appear fleetingly in a Bergman film or a line of poetry; luminous, yet defying definition and serving merely as a portal to dreaming.

In the second analysis we realized that Ernst's affective life bridged the sensorial and the verbal. At first he imagined violent actions against others, then he moved into the verbal symbolic order by occasionally

Somatoforms

speaking angrily to people, although fortunately such outbursts were tempered. I stated that he was in search of relationships, and that for him a bad relation was better than no relation at all. He found this idea stunning. It had never occurred to him that he was seeking friendships through his imagined scenes of violence.

It is a critical moment in the analysis of a schizophrenic person when he begins to understand the tactics he has been using to protect himself, because at this point the urge to retreat back into sensorial life is huge. We recollected the time in the first analysis when Ernst showed up in my consulting room one day with an awful mohawk haircut. One side was blue, the other red. In addition he had painted his face and looked like some wandering football fan who had become lost on his way home from the stadium. At the time, he seemed completely uninterested in my surprise.

I said that in retrospect he seemed to have found a way to resolve the problematic between living entirely in the realm of the imaginary and moving into language. I said that I thought he had exported his own use of language as a purely intrasubjective phenomenon; now I was to have inner conversations with myself over what I saw in him. He was forcing others into being like himself: a person who could converse with others only if they were mental objects, so he could supply all the language, like internal voice-overs.

He agreed. He told me that he spent a lot of time watching himself and commenting on himself as an outside observer might. In his imagination he evaluated each and every one of his possible gestures, and he apologized if he had a similar effect on me. I said that, intriguingly, I did often find myself wondering about whether I should or should not say certain things to him, but that when I did speak it usually felt natural.

We mused on the shared experience of our internal imagined encounters with each other, on the relations between our respective

I and me as we each conversed internally and imagined our selves in the room, engaged in potential communication with the other. It was a world of withheld discourse, one not lost upon the self, and we noted that these imaginary relationships and conversations were in fact attempts to share self with other, to move toward speaking and engaging.

It was clear to me that, after many years of our working together, Ernst had made a decision that he would teach me about himself. I was no longer just an analyst per se; I was now a student being taught by a master in his own art form. This was a brilliant strategy that aimed to defeat the hazards of mental life while finding a way to live.

Ernst found the sensorial realm irritating, but other schizophrenics form very different relationships to the world of their origins. Some cast the sensorial into higher sensoriform articulations.

In Winnicott's phrase "the environment mother"—a wonderfully simple wording—lies centuries of wisdom. The environment mother relates only partly to the world the actual mother sets up. It consists of all the impressing presentations from the real that originate from both outside and inside the newborn. This is the infant's experience before and after feeding, sleeping, urination, and defecation. The environment can transport the self, sometimes to good places, sometimes not so good. In this environment, the body can sing its seemingly electric connection to the outside world, or be sucked back to visceral inner urges.

Throughout life we are sensory and will often continue to somatize lived experience. Sometimes something that would ordinarily be the object of thought and speech is denied and rerouted through the body for sensory process. A patient who suffered intense spousal abuse endured years of severe stomach cramps. Her psychiatrist warned her that somatization of her conflict made her liable to serious physical consequences. Sadly, she developed a cancer. The world of psychosomatics will involve most therapists, at one time or another, in the logic of somatization. The aim of psychotherapy is to reverse this process and to analyze *somatic liability* (the patient's unconscious preference for somatizing rather than symbolizing) in order to help spare the body the consequences of diverted mental distress.

The schizophrenic opts for a more radical move: he returns to sensorial experience, not simply to somatize conflict but to shift *all* mental processes into a somatic alternative. So rather than allowing himself feelings of annoyance with a dinner guest, Ernst transferred such thoughts into irritation with the lighting in the hallway. Had he been asked what he felt about the guest he would have responded "I don't know," and this would have been true.

In one transformative session during the second analysis I was struck by his repeated use of the word "painful." He began the hour telling me that he had found the early morning birdsong a "pain." The soap in his shower was "abrasive." He was also pained by articles of clothing and did not feel comfortable in what he was wearing. He had gone outdoors, but "people in general" were "a pain" and he had imaginary conversations with them.

I said it was curious that the word "pain" could apply to the body as well as to the mind; one could be pained by an itch and scratch the skin to resolve the problem, or one could be pained by a person and get annoyed with them in order to externalize the feeling. We spent time discussing the movement from the many somatic irritants he felt to the affective pains that pursued him through the day.

We all move from our sensorial foundations to affective derivatives and eventually to the symbolic transformations of verbal language. With the self in dire straits, the schizophrenic returns to sensorial life, abandoning the symbolic order and mental life, which has become a terrifying realm. He then resides in a suspended state between senso-riform communication and inner speech, rarely risking a return to the symbolic order except to utter words that are thinglike: to be spat out or taken in rather than acting as vehicles for communicating thoughts.

16

Dumbing Down

INFANTS AND TODDLERS are mothered and fathered in fatefully impressive ways. Good or not, parents suffuse an infant's being and influence the course of a lifetime.

In their ordinary everyday acts (physical, verbal, and emotional) parents communicate theories of how we should eventually parent ourselves. In all respects they are responding to us, so a set of unconscious instructions bears our mark upon them.

After all, we are all ingenues. Although the parents are the nominal experts, and most kids take parent-generated laws to be models for self-development, they are adapting to who we are and each of us is a parental "one off" for better or worse.

One way or another, we evolve techniques for nurturing ourselves, according to our situation and age, that may echo or symmetrically oppose the maternal: we soothe ourselves in tough situations, we tell ourselves tomorrow is another day and to rest up and get a good night's sleep, we feed ourselves food that is comforting. We also father ourselves: enjoining ourselves to face up to reality, to try harder, to abandon self-pity and get organized. This may reflect our actual father's way of fathering us, or more likely it will be a mix of our original idiom, axioms determined by the father, and our inter-pretive alteration of paternal patterns.

Putting the Oedipus complex aside for the moment, when our psyche has *structuralized* the mother's and father's orders, then rather than actively imagining what they might say, do, or not do to help us deal with an issue, we just get on with it.

Before the child is bewildered by sexual difference and the role of the father, he is shocked by the arrival of genital sexual excitement. This is a disruption derived, not from competition with the parent of the opposite sex, but by a natural evolution in the child's own body and mind. Since these feelings are unprecedented, body and mind seem conjoined in a logic that is bewildering to the self.

Children abandon the Oedipus complex (or should we term it the "family complex"?), not because they are exhausted by the struggle or because marriage to the parent of choice is forbidden, but because the initial promise of housing one's desire in the mother or father is annihilated by the disturbing encounter with group life. In this respect I differ with the Lacanian argument that it is adherence to the sym-bolic order (the rules of language, society, and conscious linear think-ing) that separates the child from the mother and prepares the self for participation in the social world. This is true, but only up to a point, and it is what occurs after that demarcation that is crucial in under-standing psychoses.

In "Why Oedipus?" I argued that although we might wish for the logic of the symbolic order to rescue us from psychosis, we find that the reality of group life usurps the way father has ordered our family.[1] The psychological forces implicit in any group process can easily defeat the laws of society, rules of culture, or linguistic sense. In other words, groups can go mad; and if we need any validation of the ease with which the symbolic order can be pushed to the side

Dumbing Down

we only need look at the dark side of humanity—homicide, genocide, war, and the everyday callous indifference to the plight of
others.

Instruction in the psychology of groups begins very early. At the
same time the school-age child is discovering that the world is not fair,
that friends can turn into enemies at the drop of a hat, he also learns
that his own mind is not simply a comfy zone for the transmission of
benign views. The potential for hatred of mothers, fathers, and others
is deeply disturbing. Efforts at reparation are never entirely successful. Envy of friends' accomplishments, and triumph at their failures,
compete in the mind with the sense of the ethical and the good. In
short, we discover that mental life is its own group process, one that
does not recognize rules.

Of course, each individual deals with this convergent crisis in
childhood in his own particular way, but there are general human
reactions to all of this. We retreat from conscious knowledge of the
complexity of both forms of group life: in the outside world and in
our minds. We dumb ourselves down, opting for simple versions of
reality, and for the solace of good friendships that, as long as they last,
console us against the anxiety of complexity. We construct a life-
sustaining illusion that we are safe, that goodness prevails in both the
external and the internal worlds.

Although we know that bad things happen in reality—a person can
be knocked off his bike, a tornado can rip a house apart, a burning cig-
arette can set a sofa on fire—these seem like out-takes. We generally
sustain the view that although things can go wrong, they tend not to.
News of events such as genocide, thousands of people slaughtered by
other human beings, are described as "unimaginable" or "inhuman"
or "beyond belief." We simply cannot accept that most people are
indeed capable of murder and that such apparent aberrations are as

representative of the human race as the building of a church or a society coming together to clean up a city after a hurricane.

It may well be that this illusion is a phylogenetic necessity, one that needs us to make use of denial in order to live within the illusion.

In view of the schizophrenic's capacity to distort reality, it is an irony that his vulnerability renders him incapable of the forms of denial employed by the normal person. In order to be normal we must lessen our conscious realization of the complexity, both of our own minds—how they shift in the internal representation of our moods and views of others—and of participation in group life. By joining in with this collective diminishment of intrapsychic and group reality, most people get along adequately within their life span, even enduring profound hardships without breaking down.

Schizophrenics are often precocious as children, frequently speaking early and developing language skills to a very high order. They also tend to be devout adherents to the laws of society, obsessional about being part of the social order. If anything, they would seem to be exemplars of the symbolic order. They are often articulate, gifted isolates who may amass unusual expertise (often in scientific areas) very early in their development, putting mental life and academic achievement before intimate social encounters. What they lack is a kind of emotional intelligence; a relaxed and sentient relatedness to others.

Looked at this way, it seems that schizophrenia begins with an inability to live generatively within the maternal order. The terms of life in that order include communication through a variety of spontaneous emotional connections; the projection of greed, rage, anxiety, and other affects into the object world for containment and transformation into sustainable emotions; and the ability to encounter the object world as a good thing that impresses the self in creatively divergent ways so that the self can enjoy the thingness of the world. These are the unconscious processes that enable one to develop a core that can trust its communications, both with things and with people.

The schizophrenic suffers core ontological anxieties, as R. D. Laing put it, unsure of how to be receptive to the thingness of the world, or to play with reality. Although he may feel at home with structured games routed through the symbolic order, he is awkward in self-to-other engagements.

I have discussed some of the ways in which schizophrenics try to eliminate both disturbing mental contents and the mental processes that bring these into consciousness. The aim is to protect the self against the hazards of mind. I have proposed that they develop a hybrid form of being, a compromise between adult and infant levels of functioning. In a previous chapter I described how they may elect to revert to a type of sensorial existence. It is a common observation that, following their breakdown, schizophrenics seem highly sensitive to color, light, and sound. This is because they are now organizing reality according to a particular type of proprioceptive skill. The body and its being seem like a safe haven from the mind and its thought processes. For Freud, the first ego is a body ego, and it is as if the schizophrenic has returned, in a highly sophisticated form, to this position.

Another way of putting it is that the schizophrenic seeks a world to inhabit that is not mediated by the mind but apprehended by the senses and the realms of bodily being.

When people become untrustworthy, physical objects (both animate and inanimate) can become substitutes for self-other relating. At this point the connection between the self and the object world is, at its core, a sensorial one: the self is engaged in an inter-sensual relation with the world. Schizophrenics may become experts on particular physical objects—it might be a tree or a rock formation—but this interest is not an intellectually learned one. They will talk about the object as they have come to know it through its physical immanence, as if it has almost sacred properties. They know these properties through a new form of intuition that puts them in touch with the physical world in a highly sensitized way.

The schizophrenic sense of intuition is rather remarkable. Having reverted to sensorial proprioceptive perception, he is unknowingly making use of complex unconscious perceptions. Consciousness is not an intermediary here; indeed, the self becomes almost completely devoid of circuits of thought and instead seems connected directly to the real, conveying its essence to the other through various forms of apparently mystically driven communication: humming, curious sentence formations, and gestures.

Within the maternal order, mother and infant communicate sensorially. Language proper will be used by the mother, but for the infant her words form a complex sound system that transmits attitudes and unconscious emotions. The mother's facial sign system is a highly complex pictorial (or hieroglyphic) representation of the world. The smells of the mother, and those that emanate from her world, are another subtle system of inter-sensual indications. The capacity of mother and infant to impress one another through these coordinate streams of unconscious sensorial communication builds up a powerful sense in each of being in intuitive contact. When things go well the self may take this as a foundation for all future knowledge; indeed, there will be great reluctance to have this knowledge mitigated by verbal communication.

In order to return to the sensorial, schizophrenics go through a process of designification in which they strip language of its signifying function. Observers have noted that they seem to concretize language, or skew it into some private neologistic enterprise, or use it only on rare occasions, stripped of compound sentence structure, reduced to a simplified vocabulary.

What I think is often missed is the logic of this designification.

The schizophrenic is actually sensationalizing language, turning its signifying function into a sense-property so that words are divided up into categories of pleasure or pain. If a word is deemed to be saturated with mental pain it is removed from the lexicon, but if it is a safe word it may be used often, in a seemingly talismanic way. Words become things.

However, it would be a mistake to conclude that, having done this to language, the schizophrenic can no longer use words in the same way as the rest of us. This would be akin to deciding that Picasso's cubist representations of women eradicated his ability to draw a figurative portrait. In fact, designification does not mean that schizophrenics cannot use language and, more important, it does not mean they do not understand us when we speak to them.

PART THREE

17

Where Are *You* From?

WHEN I WRITE AS AN "I" in the first person pronoun, it is crucial to my act of thinking and speaking that I take this position for granted. I am speaking "for myself," and even if what I say may be full of contradictions—indeed to the point of bringing into question whether I actually have any right to this I—it would be impossible for me to think and speak unless I spoke myself from this position.

The I is crucial. The act of speaking for oneself sustains the essential illusion of a continuous perspectival authority. Although one's point of view will shift all the time, based on both internal and external phenomena, the I is a psychic position that reflects the integrative function of the ego as it unconsciously perceives, organizes, and communicates unconscious processes. As the representative of the ego in consciousness, the I occupies a unique position, in that it reflects the strengths and contradictions of one's unconscious organization (the ego) and one's unconscious thinking.

As we have seen, in schizophrenic breakdown the integrity of the I is fragmented and projected into the environment for safekeeping. The pronominal presence may remain in a superficial way, but much else is lost. For example, the self's capacity to think with ordinary logic may seem to disappear. If we ask a schizophrenic what he would do if he found himself in a small boat at sea, he might say he would change the sea into land and get rid of the boat. The fact that this does not make realistic sense is unimportant to him. He is interested only in driving off thoughts that cannot be contained by an I that is no longer around to organize them, to think them, and to speak them.

Narrating the self invariably strengthens the I. As well as being informative in itself, the simple act of talking and talking and talking, recounting in minute detail the events of the previous days, is structurally efficacious. As the I speaks, again and again, it resumes its representative function. Consciousness begins its return to the self.

Any person who is dissolved by schizophrenia must be given substantial amounts of time to speak, to utter the word "I," in order to feel the restoration of the narrative core. When the patient speaks to the analyst, the clinician proceeds to link emotional states to actual events (symbolic nodal points), and the patient has a chance to become recontextualized, returned to the historical self. He then avoids being left to invent a new person and a new myth.

Part of the cure lies in narrating the quotidian. Ordinarily I will simply ask the person to tell me what has happened in the days leading up to the moment when he changed. This is an act of diligent searching for the butterfly moment when the patient felt his reality shift. Going back to painful events is crucial to the restoration of the self. For example, if it concerns moving house or school, the patient needs to recall in detail what he loved about the home he had to abandon, or his experiences in the school where he felt connected with his friends.

For Josef Breuer and Sigmund Freud the "talking cure" was the medium of therapeutic transformation for the neurotic. The argument proposed here is that talking soon after a psychotic breakdown can help reverse the schizophrenic process, because it implicitly restores the narrative hegemony of the I. As patient and analyst go over the details of what took place in the recent past, this act of historicity and narrativity becomes the glue that restores the self and prevents further splitting and fragmentation.

If comparatively few clinicians have experienced this reversal of the schizophrenic process, this is because the crucial act of regaining context through taking a history and the function of returning the self to narrative activity have not been high on the list of clinical priorities. Instead the patient loses contact with his mind through heavy medication and is separated from narrative coherence because no one allows him to talk. Tragically, the treatment he receives becomes a crucial agent in cementing the schizophrenic process.

With the schizophrenic, engaging his I, the subjective position, is crucial. If he has not given up, there is time to get him to shore. If he does give up and is drowning in a psychotic process, he may be revived by medication, but he will not be the person one could have reached before this self-abandonment and fragmentation.

In the days after breakdown a person usually wants to talk and is reachable. If days give way to weeks and months and no one is there to talk to—intensely, deeply, madly, and at length—then all involved are in a different realm. The need to talk and to find help has not been met. The patient has been abandoned to another order and is now lost to what we term schizophrenia.

The task facing the clinician becomes very difficult when this happens. Whereas the exploratory, narrative-based approach that is used immediately following an acute breakdown bears a close resemblance to a technique based on free association, what is required when schizophrenia has become entrenched within the self might appear to be a radical departure from familiar practice.

Where Are You From?

171

I have discussed how the schizophrenic's initial response after the apocalypse may be to befriend the voices and to diminish the mind so as to avoid the arrival of disturbing mental contents, or he may fight the voices and try to hide the self away. There are many tactics that serve this strategy, and I have considered some of them, including the process of disinhabitation, in which mental functions are placed into physical objects, both for safekeeping and in order to distance them from the self.

Soon, however, he will be devoted to forming a new world constituted around hallucinogenic realities, fearing that those around him may try to interfere with this enterprise. It will come as no surprise that, at this point, he may be reluctant to be in contact with a clinician, or with anyone who wants to examine his internal world. By this time he has become organized against introspection, because to look within the self, from his point of view, is to invite the catastrophe of the arrival of thoughts. When thoughts do arrive he will attempt to encrypt them in omnipotently guided codes that give him the sense that he is in charge of the thought process. He may sense that the therapist is covertly aiming to remove him from this new world that is protecting him from catastrophe.

One aim of analysis, therefore, is to ease the defenses employed by the schizophrenic against the fantasy of annihilation and to replace them with nurturant realities that offset anxiety with assurances, both from the clinician and from the person's own strengthened self.

Since at first the patient may be frightened of any attention being directed toward his mind, the analyst may want to introduce third-object phenomena that are not interrogative. This creates a third area, a zone of comparative safety in which it will be possible to make contact with the patient. Importantly, and contrary to conventional free associative technique, this object will be introduced by the psychologist. He might initiate a discussion of events that happened the previous day, or mention a film that the patient has seen, or comment on a political issue or a celebrity figure. Whether discussing Harry Potter, a well-known TV presenter, or the menu at the hospital, the clinical challenge is to make use of such objects to transform defensive fear into intersubjective engagement.

Schizophrenics in hospitals are often left alone in the dense, thick silence of a psychotic universe. Before we can expect them to talk to others, they will need to hear therapists talking to them.

Initially, the schizophrenic will usually regard any relationship as highly dangerous—it will evoke affect and mental content, and is therefore liable to elicit psychotic anxieties. However, after working in this way for some time, psychologists generally encounter *schizophrenic curiosity*. The person may become curious about the therapist.

One patient said later that when he first began to work with me it was like watching TV, except that I was real. Then one day, after a few weeks of silence, he suddenly said: "You talk funny." After a while he asked, "Where are you from?" We could say that he had noticed my mid-Atlantic accent and that he genuinely did not know where I came from. But these queries also represent an unconscious question. He is asking not "Who are you?" but "What world do you come from?"

He may have denuded the self of its human dimension, but now he encounters a human being in the room, one who reveals the self's inner life, who plays with objects of thought, and who links thought to reality. For the schizophrenic, this is a strange being. From curiosity about what the analyst is, the patient shifts to noticing certain traits about him. These might include the therapist's syntactical idiom (the way he words language), his sonic presence (tones of voice, inflexions), his physical distinctiveness (his forms of gesture, of being embodied) or his particular ways of engaging the other through visual, sonic, and proprioceptive skills.

Where Are You From?

This curiosity may take months or years to develop, and with some patients it may never happen. But if the psychologist has engaged the patient soon enough after the breakdown, then there is a fair chance that it will develop, and when it does it is an important step in their human relations. Patient and analyst meet at a crossroads: can they develop curiosity about each other, or are they to remain as fortified islands of independence, simply passing commonalities back and forth?

After a while, the patient may abandon the schizophrenic gaze and no longer use the optical black hole to rid the self of here-and-now experience. He may begin to listen to the analyst and take in what is said. If and when curiosity segues into affection, this marks another important moment in the evolution of the relationship. It is a subtle but discernible step. Over time, the patient finds the therapist's traits reliable, then reassuring, then somewhat amusing, and finally endearing.

This is the basis of nonpsychotic love, and it brings an enormous relief to the patient, but also potential danger. It is not psychotic empathy, where the schizophrenic fuses with the other whom he has fallen in love with; we have discussed the ways in which he may go about hiding his mind in order to protect himself from this kind of fusion. The analyst's difference indicates that he is not available for empathic fusion; indeed, it is his absolute, idiomatic otherness that is the object of interest and then affection. This is part of the self's discovery of the integrity of an object, its distinctness, and this promotes *perceptive identification* as an alternative to projective identification.[1] Since it would be terrifying to the schizophrenic to project anything into a human being, the analyst's task is to offer his own self-observations as perceivable-in-themselves.

During this period of curiosity and then affection, the clinician will begin, from time to time, to make interpretations. At first these will be directed at alienating moments when the patient is made anxious by the therapist. At this point it is sufficient simply to identify the alarm and to indicate empathy for the person's fear.

For many months, Mark said nothing. He would sit in silence, sometimes rotating his head to the left in an android way and focusing his gaze on the windowsill. I did not comment on this. Then one day he said, "Do you hear it?" I thought he was referring to a hallucination, and I asked, "Did I hear what?" He replied, "The fly." I said no, I had not heard it, and at first I assumed there must be a fly in the room. And then I heard myself corrected by my own inner voice, which said something like "No—there is *a fly on the wall*." From that inner association I realized that he might be saying that I was a fly on the wall, listening to what he had to say and spying on him. When I said this to him it brought a big smile to his face and he indicated that I had understood his previously enigmatic communication. Being understood by me did not feel to him like an impingement, because by then he had decided that I was a heck of an odd fellow and it was just his lot to have been thrown in with me.

Because of his amusement at my associative comments, Mark gradually began to tell me about some of his own "interests." He was interested in automobiles from the 1950s. He might ask, for example, whether I had seen the 1955 Plymouth around town that week. He would then tell me in great detail everything one could possibly want to know about this particular car.

Such objects are not amalgam-things, but distinctively integral objects that have their own identity and are part of the human collective. His interest in them may have been previously hidden away for fear that it might be stolen from him.

People working with autistic children and adults will note the similarity here. For the psychotic person, safe knowledge is knowledge about a specific object, usually one that has mechanical properties or

is in some way a reliable and neutral phenomenon. It does not function as the receptacle for projective identifications; instead it allows
the self to engage in perceptive identification that is not invaded by
hallucinatory thinking. We might think of this as a form of transitional object that permits the self to invest interest in a non-human
object with human passion. By sharing that object with the analyst,
the schizophrenic is gradually coming out of his enclave and risking
disclosure of the very thing that most concerns him. This is a precious moment, as it represents the reemerging of the life instinct that
has been sequestered for safekeeping.

Even at this point, he may still defend against the apocalypse by
using android speech. By changing his previous sonic, syntactical, and
gestural idioms to a mechanical delivery, he divests communication of
the human dimension. That quality may never leave him. He may
always retain vestiges of the android speaker to protect him against
the hazards of human emergence. This defense is a secret that I think
for the most part needs to be respected by the clinician and not drawn
attention to. The form of the schizophrenic's speech is under the auspices of a false self that is protecting the true self from annihilation.

The schizophrenic's interest in the analyst's idiom, which is experienced initially as rather strange and foreign, heralds the slow rediscov-
ery of his former self, the human self that has been lost. To encounter
the idiomatic subjectivity of the psychologist, revealed through affec-
tionate free speech, is to assimilate slowly, through observation and
then identification, the ordinary features of human sensibility.

I used to wonder whether my patients knew this was what I was
doing when speaking my thoughts and interests out loud, but they
never indicated whether they did or did not. When working with
schizophrenics, many aspects must remain as secrets. It is as if restoration of the self can take place only if it is taken into account that the

schizophrenic is in hiding because he lives in a dangerous world, one in which he thinks it is best to go about finding his personality, his family, and his culture without anyone noticing.

As I have stated, there is a big difference between working with a person who is just undergoing a schizophrenic breakdown and one who has suffered the catastrophe some time ago and is well into the schizophrenic position. I have focused on how one works, initially, with the schizophrenic who will fend off any clinical encounter. What about the person who is experiencing the first manifestations of the schizophrenic process?

Here the analyst will work differently. This is the time to pose questions and try to elicit specific information. In particular, one must "take a history."

It might be thought that asking a schizophrenic to go over the events of the previous days or weeks would be invasive. But in very much the same way that Freud saw how the seemingly irrelevant trivia of the everyday in the process of free association revealed far more than the felt deep disturbances in one's being, if the psychoanalyst is able to take a history soon after a schizophrenic's collapse it can become a vital matrix in recovery.

This is not news to those working in the therapies of schizophrenics. In Finland one approach has been to ask all members of the family to attend family sessions to begin with. The question to be discussed: "What has happened in the last year"? These clinicians know that it is crucial to the understanding of the schizophrenic to discover what particular event set off the transition to schizophrenia.

Before coming to the work of history, let us reflect on the odd fact that, for most of us, the rich experience of each day becomes dulled by the morrow that displaces it, as present-time epiphanies—vivid experiences of sensing and knowing—move into "the past." The death of each day is essential if we are not to become overwhelmed by our human being.

Schizophrenics suffer an arrest in this essential distancing of the meaning of the everyday. They can become deranged by a single event.

When we take a history and ask what has happened in the past to disrupt the self, it invariably seems rather ordinary. This is because the significance lies not in the event itself, but in the fact that one day's event has pursued the self, unaltered, into the next day. And into the next. This is not memory; it is a radical mental intrusion into the self's going-on-being. Something in the psychic spatio-temporal calibration of the self's requirements for functioning is derailed.

In normality we live with the illusion that we foresee the future, or at least a range of future possibilities. We prepare ourselves for being let down or socially chided. We carry the assumption that a well-prepared self is a safe haven, and the illusion of safety in the present has implications for how we look back on the past. If something upsets our apple cart, challenging our certainty that the present is safe, then we are unlikely to want to revisit that experience.

But in schizophrenia it seems that the self has not, consciously or unconsciously, perceived the possibility of the event.

A woman hosts a party for thirty people, but a lapse in planning means there is only food and cutlery for twenty-five. An adolescent football quarterback throws a pass too far for his end in the dying sec-onds of his team's valiant effort to come back from a great deficit. They lose.

These are shocking moments.

Most people will rebound, but not all. Some are hijacked by a shock in the past that becomes an eternal present. The self is suspended, remaining on a constant watch, and this means they can no longer inhabit everyday reality. Past-present-future ceases to have any meaning. The temporal structures of being are lost.

We are in a different territory.

The analytical function of "history taking," then, is not simply an attempt to think about and interpret the past—it is the restoration of human temporality itself. The simple act of asking after what happened returns the patient to that day when the event unfolded. And in so doing it invites the shock to return, the affects to recur, and the self's breakdown to become clearly apparent.

Taking a history is also oddly consoling. When I meet a schizophrenic for the first time we are both anxious. Almost always this person is in some very extreme state, and it can be quite frightening to be in the room. I did not give much thought, in my early clinical days, to why I took a history. I just did it. It was only after a few decades that I realized something important: going into the recent past and asking the person to tell me what he had been doing, step-by-step, was something we could do *together*.

We could pause and chat during such a dialogue. "Oh, so you went to see the film *Boyhood*? Amazing stuff." These "breaks" are relaxing, allowing two ordinary people to chew on the spices of life.

But there is something else to doing this: it begins to establish a state of reverie.

Working together to recover the facts of the everyday begins to morph into a dreamlike chronology, almost as if the day residue is already moving toward the dream proper that may come later that night. The psychoanalyst and the schizophrenic find refuge in the everyday, they begin to benefit from the reverie intrinsic to indexing that day, and then, almost every single time, out of this dreaming-the-day together *the event* pops up. "And then I realized that there were plates and food only for twenty-five people and I just, you know . . ."

"My God, how awful, of course."

The reverie that is history has not only transformed the inchoate nature of the past by putting it into a shared narrative; it has generated a receptive attitude in the mind so that the emotional experience that shocked the self into a schizophrenic reaction can be accessed. It is impossible to describe how meaningful this is to both persons. There is no need for celebration or emphasis. The recalled event has already spoken for itself in the here and now, and from this point forward analyst and patient will work from a shared emotional epiphany that binds them together in a deeply moving search for the meanings behind that event and why it was so deeply disturbing.

Part Three

18

Change

WE SHALL NEVER KNOW whether schizophrenia is the outcome of phylogenetic, genetic, intra-uterine, early infantile, infant-mother, linguistic, sex shock, family, or accident-in-the-real causes. Clearly it is yet another form of being human.

However, we do know something about how schizophrenics perceive reality, how they think, how they behave, and how they relate. We know a great deal about why they resist many forms of treatment, but we also know how, why, and when they seem prepared to work with a clinician.

Whatever the genesis of schizophrenia, the first distinct outcome is a split in the self in which one part functions in an ordinary manner and another part develops a radically different way of perceiving, thinking, and relating.

The emerging alternative changes many of the self's unconscious axioms of being. The ordinary axioms of the mind are those para digms of perceptual organization that are generated by innate features of the human species and those acquired in the course of human relations, especially in the first year of life. We are governed by thousands of unthought known axioms that we never think because they formed before we had concepts with which to think them, when our idiom met with thousands of experiences that established our unconscious decisions about how to be and relate.

It would be impossible to provide an inclusive index of the axioms that govern mental structure, but in psychoanalysis and psychotherapy some become available for knowing.

To give one simple example, we believe that we are separate from the objects that we perceive around us. If I walk down a street and see a car I assume I see something that is not myself. The car and I are distinctly different phenomena.

A schizophrenic might see a car and assume that the car is a part of the self. If the car is a Volvo and the schizophrenic a female who believes her vulva organizes her orientation to reality, then the sight of a Volvo might be experienced as a manifestation of her vulva. Because of designification and the return from the symbolic to the sensorial order, words are often used by schizophrenics because of their sound meaning. Vulva is close in sound to Volvo.

This simple equation—Volvo is my vulva—would be one axiom governing this person's relation to reality that constitutes a part of her mental structure. Likewise, "stream" is close to "scream"; a schizophrenic might elect to scream at someone by yelling the word "stream."

Mental structure is composed of countless assumptions that constitute the predicates of mind.

When I am engaged to help change the mental structure of a schizophrenic, I begin by trying to identify those axioms that constitute their psychotic assumptions. I then put them into words in order to change their status from that of a given to that of a view.

Psychotherapy of the schizophrenic works through the careful personal anthropology of the individual's core convictions, those that seem to govern his mentality. This book has outlined the many differing preconditions for the effectiveness of interpretations, especially the crucial role of the analyst's way of listening, his empathy, and his basic human presentation. At some point, however, he will begin to analyze disturbed axioms in order to effect structural change.

The process is strikingly simple even if often it takes many months or years. Take the example of the woman who merges with a Volvo.

Once the clinician understands that a Volvo is the patient's vulva, he can simply say so. By putting an axiom into words the analyst changes the status of the axiom. It is no longer part of the unthought known. It has now been *subjected* to thought. I emphasize the word "subjected" because it is now a way of addressing the function of the subject in life and in analysis. Broadly speaking, the subject is the felt agent of our mentality. In psychoanalysis and other psychologies it refers to our identity as conscious beings, so that when I use the pronoun "I," this basic assumption is not to be challenged. As I speak, I do so as the verbal representative of my being.

When the clinician puts the equation "Volvo is my vulva" into speech, it enters consciousness. This is not to say that the schizophrenic has been unconscious of this assumption; indeed, she (or it could be a he) may have consciously thought that a Volvo was a body part. But when the psychoanalyst puts it into speech and enters it into the consciousness shared between analyst and patient, it becomes objectified as a topic of, and for, thinking.

If the clinician is sensitive and does not attempt to prise this axiom from the patient's being—if he or she is thoughtful—then thinking out loud through interpretation and conversation is not experienced by the schizophrenic as endangering.

For example, the analyst might say, "It is easier to think of your vulva if you locate it in a Volvo." This helps the person grasp the meaning of this transfer, and comprehension reverses the agency of meaning. She is no longer the *recipient* of such an equation. She now understands it, and she is then free either to retain it as an assumption, or the memory of one, or to abandon it.

I am not asserting that such an observation is in itself the agent of transformation—it is merely a hermeneutic step in altering the assumption—but it is effective because it provides a localized meaning. This implicitly makes an axiom conditional, *because* it was a meaning that had become an assumption. The understanding of its local meaning and then its wider ramifications—the Volvo was a part of her body moving in the object world, available for genital incorporation of objects, and so forth—constitute a potential space.

Any good interpretation that makes an unconscious assumption conscious creates a potential space. The potential is that through wording and understanding, a previous axiom can now change, transformed by the relief delivered through that understanding and its withstanding of many challenges to it over time.

Consciousness in this moment is transitional. It resides for a period of time between the analysand's former unconscious assumptions and new ones resulting from the work of psychotherapy. The test of more lasting change will be whether the patient continues to equate Volvo with vulva or whether this assumption is relinquished in the face of reality.

In the work of ordinary psychoanalysis or psychotherapy, when the analyst makes an interpretation it will be a mental object usually associated with the analyst. If the patient agrees with it, it may continue to be associated with the analyst and remain an introject. This will of course affect the way the patient thinks about the object of thought, but it does not yet mean that he has changed. Indeed, when a patient says, "I was about to say something to my mother when all of a sudden your voice came into my mind and I decided not to," the patient is indicating that the analyst's effectiveness is partial.

It is only when the analysand changes her mental position and her behavior, no longer referring to the analyst but now presenting her new point of view as her own, that we know the conscious interpretation has become a new axiom in the mind. This is what is meant by *structuralization*. Something put into words, objectified in the transitional fields of consciousness, held within the patient as an internal object of thought associated with the analyst, is now assimilated into the patient's mind. It is a new form within the self's unconscious.

When working with a schizophrenic, core axioms exist that need transformation through interpretation. (I have discussed many of those in this book, for example the axioms of metasexuality, animism, projective identification, and senselessness). Ordinarily a time will arrive when the patient is ready to think about one or another of these core action-thoughts. As with any patient, it may be months or years before this process of thought—in which unconscious assumptions are placed in the potential space inherent to consciousness—brings about change.

What proof do we have that the person is no longer schizophrenic? The evidence resides in the altered assumptions that now govern this person's mental life and behavior. It is not a question of adding something to the self that was missing; it is a matter of transforming a psychotic axiom into its non-psychotic alternate.

The process is not mysterious but quite ordinary. As infants become toddlers, many axioms change. The assumption that food arrives if we cry is eventually replaced by the notion that in order to get food we must speak. As we grow older that recognition will change to a realization that in order to eat something we may have to get the food for ourself from the refrigerator or cupboard. In adolescence and then in adult life, axioms will alter again, as we come to realize that in order to get food we need to earn money, go to the stores, purchase the food, prepare it at home, and so forth.

In other words, although we are governed by axioms, they alter over time. We are thus unconsciously accustomed to notional change: to restructuralizations of the mind. Indeed this simple, inevitable fact of human mental life is the foundation of any success to be found in clinical psychoanalysis.

Unfortunately, for whatever reasons, schizophrenics have found many of those ordinary changes traumatic, and a vital condition of therapeutic effectiveness will be whether the analyst can reintroduce the analysand to the generative potential of change. He will have to earn the person's trust that the trauma of change has some benefit to it.

As with any analysand, once this happens, then one does not need to analyze individually all the disturbed assumptions that govern a mind. One of the intriguing facts of clinical work is that once the therapist has analyzed several of the core assumptions, then it is as if the mind recalibrates other disturbed axioms, and an endogenous intrapsychic change takes place.

This is most vividly noticed in work with adolescents. For example, an anorectic who is functioning, let us say, according to many disturbed axioms may transform all of them as the result of a single axiomatic change. One such axiom—"I suffer an illness called anorexia that has taken me over and I can do nothing about it," say— might be subjected to the interpretation "You prefer to call the change from being a child to becoming an adult an illness, because you are distressed by inevitable changes in your body." Over time, if this interpretation is accepted by the analysand, then she may not only emerge from the anorectic behavior, but many other assumptions about being and relating may be unconsciously transformed as well.

Schizophrenics too can embark on many changes as a result of intensive psychotherapy, but such changes will take longer for them than for the non-psychotic personality. Although medications may prove invaluable in the course of psychotherapy, nothing helps schizophrenics more than a single one-on-one commitment by a fellow human being who has taken the time and endured the training to know how to read them, be with them, understand them, and talk to them.

19

Lucy on an Island

FIFTEEN MILES FROM PEKIN, North Dakota, the straight paved roads give way to river valleys and rolling hills. Highways yield to county gravel roads and then to dirt tracks that lead to farmsteads hidden by woodland. Set against the rolling grassland of the prairie, the trees seem like skyscrapers. In winter the northern woods protect homes from Alberta Clippers that drive the temperature down by twenty to forty degrees. The west woods meet the vast snowstorms coming from the Pacific Northwest, and the east woods bend the curving winds that come up from the Gulf of Mexico carrying snow and ice by the time they get here.

My farmstead is in a small microclimate. Facing south, I do not need to heat the house during a sunny day in the winter months, except for early in the morning and after sunset. During the growing season it is protected against the dust storms fed by farmers churning the soil to plant crops. The wind weaving its way through the trees sings many a soft song.

My consulting room is a former porch, now glass enclosed, looking out to the west woods. The winter months are snow covered, and I begin and end my day in the dark. The winter sun casts light across the meadow to the south and the woods in ways that fashion a new world every few hours. The silence is thick and supportive.

I spend half the year at the farmstead, and when I am there my clinical work is done via Skype or the telephone. Ordinarily I see my patients for periods of work in person, but there are some people who live in remote parts of the world and I may not see them more than once a year, or even less.

Lucy wrote and asked if I was prepared to give her an analysis. She lives on a remote island in a Norwegian fjord. She is a writer supported by a family trust. Her parents are deceased, she has no siblings, and she rarely speaks to the sixty or so islanders who are her neighbors.

Her companionship comes from a highly active mind devoted to endless reworkings of either memories or sudden epiphanies that demand a great deal of elaboration. When she goes down memory lane she inevitably retrieves a distressing encounter with another person. There are some recurring characters in these memories: several teachers who did not understand her, a university professor who was wonderful to her but whose wife became jealous of their relationship, a series of editors and publishers who slighted her in differing ways, and many former friends whom she had known and abandoned since childhood. Her epiphanies would be sudden brainstorms in which she saw configurations in the landscape that momentarily objectified an unknown secret about herself. A wave crashing against the cliff took the shape of her mother leaning over her crib, trying to suffocate her; a flock of birds suddenly rising high into the sky revealed a picture of her soul ascending into heaven; moss on a rock was her masculine self that jeered at her.

When Lucy phoned, she would speak nonstop. Usually she announced an agenda. "Today I am going to tell you about Sister Underwood and the day she told me that I had to write 'I cleanse my mind of evil thoughts' one hundred times on parchment in a very cold room when I was thirteen." She would launch with great passion into these accounts, and invariably they were highly detailed, involving several people with rather vivid names. I would find these hard to recall, so I had to concentrate on each tale, because in the days to come she would refer back to them. She might say, "You remember Underwood and evil, yes?" And I would have to retrieve the tale or she would plunge into great confusion: "I *did* tell you, didn't I? Or, maybe I didn't? If you don't remember, then I suppose I did not tell you, but I have a feeling I did."

At university Lucy had concentrated on Celtic and Nordic legends, and her epiphanies were often pervaded by a conviction that she had actually seen one or another of the gods or humans who figured in these tales. I knew some of these figures from my university studies, and when I let on that I knew who one of them was, she would cry out, "Oh, Christopher, thank God you know him!" as if I had confirmed that this figure did exist in some form of reality.

Lucy hallucinated many of these figures—and she would also transform real people through "memory" into phantasmagoric presences. Often she would be fleeing from them. "I know that Mrs. Applegate has heard me thinking about her and she will come here, Christopher, she will, and I don't think I can cope with her when she shows up. Where am I to put her? She will be *furious* with me for having brought her here. And what am I to say to her?"

Lucy phoned me from a landline at eight o'clock in the evening, five days a week, always on the dot. I do not think she was ever late, and to my recollection she never called me early. I often imagined her sitting next to the phone looking at her clock and dialing thirty seconds before the hour was to begin so that it rang at near perfect time. I suppose this stands out because, although I often thought of her as a force of chaos, in many ways she lived a highly regulated life. She visited the village shop each day to buy something, she collected the post every week when it was delivered to the shop, she tended her garden diligently, and she took great care in looking after the chickens she kept. Her day and her week were structured by mandates of one kind or another: cleaning out the chicken house on Monday afternoons, emptying the rain bucket on Tuesday mornings, scrubbing the kitchen floor on Wednesdays, and so forth.

Lucy had read an essay I had written on fate versus destiny, and for some reason, she told me, this touched her deeply and she decided she wanted to talk with the author of that essay, so she contacted my publisher. Interestingly, she made it clear that had I lived near the island she would not have wanted to meet with me, and that she found the prospect of speaking on the phone each day a great relief precisely because she did not have to see me. "I don't know what I would do with you. I do not like being in the presence of people. But talking is okay."

Why had Lucy decided at fifty-five to begin an analysis?

Reading my essay by chance, she did not know if this was an act of fate or her destiny. She developed numerous theories about what this meant, some woven into Nordic myths and some into her own fictions, and others a blend of both.

Her agenda for the first months of analysis was a meticulous description of her life in an alternative commune some two hundred kilometers from her island. Her descriptions were completely devoid of feeling, and she would report events—some quite dreadful— in a voice lacking any inflexion. This was all the more striking as Lucy generally spoke in rather melodic ways.

I pointed this out, and immediately she developed a theory that I did not approve of the commune. She then defended it against imagined challenges from me, although as time went on she added more details about life there that became truly worrying.

Lucy on an Island

Some disclosures were alarming and would pop up in a narrative otherwise devoted to glowing accounts of what a wonderful community it was and how transformative it had been to be in the group. When I alluded to what seemed to be difficult times in the group, she demanded that I tell her exactly what difficult times I was referring to. If I then mentioned a particular event, she would quickly reply that she had never told me this, that I was imagining things, and now she could not trust me. I would remain quiet, but Lucy would go on and on, insisting that I was talking about an event that never happened. Then, a few sessions later, she would tell me that she felt terrible and evil. She knew she had been lying when she accused me of imagining the event, but she would counter by saying that she was sure that I did not like the commune in any event and she felt she had to defend it.

It was several years before Lucy could stand by her recollections of events in the commune. At the same time, her obsessive rumination on bad memories—which I called "chewing on the negative"—diminished, and she was able to give accounts of events on her island that were pleasant. Then in one session she screamed into the phone in an indescribably haunting way. I thought the house had caught fire or something terrible had happened. I could hear her running around, screaming, "Go away. I did not do it. Please leave me alone!" Half an hour passed, and she returned to the phone. She told me that "It" had come after her. This was a reference to a dragon that had eight legs and five eyes, and was flying around her house. It had come to kill her.

I suddenly realized that in the session I had told her it was good that the bad memories were not "dragging on," and I said that I thought my use of this phrase might have brought an image of the dragon into her mind. She insisted it was real, and she was furious that I did not believe her. "Christopher, it was right here in front of me. It was breathing *fire* at me. It scorched my dress! It has nothing to do with what you said." Her scream was still echoing in my head and her refusals were adamant and infuriated, so I said little, and the session ended.

The next day Lucy accused me of having summoned the dragon.

"If you had not called for it, it would not have come. Why did you do this to me?"

"You felt I summoned it?"

"Well, you did. You said, 'Your dragon will get you.' And it did!"

"That's what you heard?"

"No. That is what you *said*. I have a perfect memory. You did this to me."

"Why would I do that?"

"Because you hate me."

"And why do I hate you?"

"Because I am hairy, I live under a large rock in the forest, and I smell like . . ."

"A dragon?"

"That's not funny."

"No . . . I . . ."

"You are upsetting me."

"Well, clearly I am doing something wrong."

"What do you mean by that?"

"Clearly I am to blame for a most horrifying event."

"Yes, so why did you do this?"

"I think you are angry with me for listening to some of your very private thoughts and you are trying to get rid of me."

"You were horrible."

"I was, and perhaps am, the dragon who drags on about things."

"You admit that, do you?"

"Yes. It's my job to do that, sort of."

"To be a dragon?"

"No, but I do go on. Psychoanalysts *are* tedious at times."

"You made me very angry with you."

"Yes, I know."

"Did you do that intentionally?"

"No, of course not."

"Then why?"

"Lucy, you pay me to analyze you. It's my job and sometimes I don't get things right."

"Why don't you get things right?"

"Well, Lucy, I . . ."

"Christopher, I like it when you tell me what you think."

"Thanks, Lucy."

This is a fragment of a session. It was, however, very typical of what went on between us for years. Lucy would construct a universe of heinous motivations and ascribe them to me. I would try to find the underlying persecutory anxiety that authored such admonitions, and now and then we were successful in tracking down the origins of her florid hallucinations to a simple idea.

For example, I was right to link the phrase "dragging on" to "dragon." She was not persecuted by the notion that she was "dragging on," but she heard the word "drag," made a link to the idea that I thought she was a drag, and as she became *incensed* about this she felt that fire was coming out of her mouth and she saw a dragon. At the same time, I had to admit that I had been dragging on about her internal world and she was probably right to protest about this.

By the end of the fifth year of our work, Lucy was no longer hallucinating and she was no longer dwelling in past memories, but she was haunted by a history of disturbance over several decades and wondered what this was about.

One day she said, "I am schizophrenic, aren't I?" She began to read up on schizophrenia, and I found it intriguing and moving that she wanted to talk about her ailment. She said she now found it comforting to be able to describe "it," even if now and then—every six months or so—she would descend back into it, chewing on the negative and recalling hallucinations, as if playing with the notion of conjuring them up. In fact, she was getting much, much better, and these forays into the past were like curious amusements.

In the final months of our collaboration she wanted me to send her pictures of my farmstead and consulting room in North Dakota, so I did. In turn she sent me photos of her cottage, her garden and chicken coop, and the small village where she lived. North Dakota had become very important to her: during a difficult spell in our work she asked if I would just, please, tell her what I saw through my window.

"I am looking at the West Wood and there is an owl in the tree."
"What kind of owl?"
"A great horned owl. It's a bit windy and the snow is blowing to the south."
"Has the owl moved?"
"No, he is still there, just sitting."
"Where is he on the tree?"

And so it would go. I would tell her about the owl, the rabbits, the deer, the eagles, the trees, the changing weather, and so on.

It is interesting that our respective landscapes—her island, North Dakota—were like comforting third objects that nourished both of us as we struggled to help her find her mind. In the last phase of our work, however, she asked for actual photographs rather than merely my narrative of what I saw. The object world had become its own thing, not subject to anyone's narration or selective perceptual judgment. My North Dakota became her North Dakota.

After recounting many "reveries" from his early childhood, W. B. Yeats concludes in his autobiography:

> I remember very little of childhood but its pain. I have grown happier with every year of life as though gradually conquering something in myself, for certainly my miseries were not made by others but were a part of my own mind.[1]

How rare and precious is this insight into the human experience. Yeats recalls how frightening his father could be, or his grandfather, and his recollections are not short of what in today's world many would term "traumatic experiences," but the events in a life, however harrowing, are nothing in comparison to what the mind can do to the self.

Indeed, it is telling that Yeats should describe what I take to be passing schizophrenic episodes when he begins to hear a voice. Over the years it would speak to him. At first it was friendly and he was rather comforted by its presence. But then it became "a voice in my head that is sudden and startling. It does not tell me what to do, but reproves me." He also saw things that did not exist; he was told that on several occasions he reported seeing "a supernatural bird in the corner of the room."[2]

We hardly question the fact that a poet "sees things," that he hears voices and writes them down to become voices in our heads. Yet poets always make us a bit anxious. Have they dipped into the waters of madness, there to see things the rest of us would dread encountering? Or has the mind-boggling realm of the child's psyche been preserved in a chamber that returns in the form of thought we call poetry?

Lucy saw figures from Norse legend and heard human voices and the sounds of the natural world in her mind. Yeats and the poets come and go between the comforting security of the everyday and the vivid realms of the dream.

Perhaps some tarry too long in the childhood imaginary, or have a mental porosity that allows the unconscious to interrupt the humdrum with voices and bizarre percepts. The resolute, structured discipline of poetry enables gifted people to descend into the depths of the imaginary, and to return through language and form in ways that allow us, in reading them, to experience the deep structures of our existence.

Perhaps the rest of us are only "normal" because we have found a way of denying, or splitting off, or ridding ourselves of troublesome imagery and ideas.

The poets may have more to teach us about schizophrenia than do psychiatry and psychopharmacology. After all, they have learned how to descend through the layers of our past, to mesh the sensorial, imaginary, and symbolic, in such a way as to convey our unconscious knowledge. Perhaps poets come close to the mental intersections experienced by the schizophrenic.

Who knows how this happens?

Who will teach us about schizophrenia in the future?

We shall have to see.

Notes

CHAPTER 1. UP AGAINST THE WALL

1. Victor Tausk, "On the Origin of the 'Influencing Machine' in Schizophrenia," *The Psychoanalytic Quarterly* 2 (1933): 519–556.

2. Christopher Bollas, *Catch Them Before They Fall: The Psychoanalysis of Mental Breakdown* (London: Routledge, 2013).

CHAPTER 2. A NATION'S MADNESS

1. Richard Hofstadter, *The Paranoid Style in American Politics* (New York: Vintage, 2008; originally published 1965).

2. Kai T. Erikson, *Wayward Puritans: A Study in the Sociology of Deviance* (New York: Wiley, 1966).

CHAPTER 3. FROZEN PSYCHOSIS

1. Jean-Luc Donnet and André Green, *L'Enfant de ça: psychanalyse d'un entretien, la psychose blanche* (Paris: Éditions de Minuit, 1973).

CHAPTER 4. FREE SPEECH

1. For an examination of the theory and use of free association in clinical practice, see Christopher Bollas, *The Evocative Object World* (London: Routledge, 2009) and *The Infinite Question* (London: Routledge, 2009).

CHAPTER 6. DIFFERENT LOGIC

1. There was an interruption for three years when I was at Austen Riggs in the United States, but I returned to this consulting room.

2. Richard Lucas, *The Psychotic Wavelength* (London: Routledge, 2012).

CHAPTER 9. LEAVING THINGS ALONE

1. Kleinian psychoanalysts have written a great deal about the effect of projective identification into the object world. Bion's concept of "bizarre objects"—that the psychotic universe is populated by hallucinated objects that seek revenge on the self—is obviously relevant to the notion that the object world is secretly "alive."

CHAPTER 12. ASSUMED KNOWLEDGE

1. Roman Jacobson, *Verbal Art, Verbal Sign, Verbal Time* (Oxford: Basil Blackwell, 1989), pp. 133, 135.

2. Ibid., p. 137.

3. Ibid., pp. 30, 29.

4. Maurice Blanchot, *The Infinite Conversation* (Minneapolis: University of Minnesota Press, 1993; originally published 1969), p. 242.

5. Ibid., p. 242.

6. Ibid., pp. 245, 243.

CHAPTER 13. HIDING THE MIND

1. Hanna Segal, "Notes on Symbol Formation," *The International Journal of Psychoanalysis* 38 (1957): 391–397.

2. James S. Grotstein, "Nothingness, Meaninglessness, Chaos, and the 'Black Hole' 1: The Importance of Nothingness, Meaninglessness, and Chaos in Psychoanalysis," *Contemporary Psychoanalysis* 26 (1990): 257–290.

CHAPTER 14. DODGING THOUGHT

1. This precedes the mind's creation of beta elements, or undigested thoughts, as described by Bion. Here the thoughts are precluded from being presented.

CHAPTER 16. DUMBING DOWN

1. Christopher Bollas, *Being a Character* (London: Routledge, 1993).

CHAPTER 17. WHERE ARE YOU FROM?

1. Christopher Bollas, *Forces of Destiny* (London: Free Associations Books, 1989); Christopher Bollas, *The Freudian Moment* (London: Karnac Books, 2007).

CHAPTER 19. LUCY ON AN ISLAND

1. William Butler Yeats, *The Autobiography of William Butler Yeats* (New York: Collier, 1965), p. 5.

2. Ibid., p. 8.

Annotated Bibliography

Alanen, Yrjö O., Manuel González de Chávez, Ann-Louise S. Silver, and
Brian Martindale. *Psychotherapeutic Approaches to Schizophrenic Psychoses*
(London: Routledge, 2009). An invaluable contemporary text that
invites authors from different continents to describe innovations in
clinical work with schizophrenics. No other work provides this kind of
overview, and it enables the reader to see a worldwide reconsideration of
schizophrenia and how the talking therapies are the treatment of choice.

Bellak, Leopold, Marvin Hurvich, and Helen K. Gediman. *Ego Functions in
Schizophrenics, Neurotics, and Normals* (New York: Wiley, 1973). A
classic text expressing an ego psychological orientation in the treatment
of psychotic people. A skillful presentation of the way ego psychology
assesses the analysand, it is a fine example of the typology of ego
strengths and weaknesses and how understanding the spectrum helps
with diagnosis and treatment plan. Chapter 23, "Treatment" (351–398),
indicates a surprising range of approaches, including role-playing by an
analyst within the patient's fantasy life in order to accomplish "a
reorganization of psychic structures" (376).

Berke, Joseph, and Mary Barnes. *Two Accounts of a Journey Through
Madness* (New York: Other Press, 2002). Berke studied and worked
with R. D. Laing at Kingsley Hall in London, and this remarkable book

is his account—along with his schizophrenic patient Mary Barnes—of
their work at Kingsley Hall. No clinical writing—of any patient—can
ever be accurate, but this book is a profound effort to capture the
visceral reality of a schizophrenic's (or perhaps psychotic hysteric's)
own reality. A profoundly gifted clinician, Berke went on to form the
Arbours Association and trained hundreds of London clinicians in his
own art of work with psychotic patients.

Boyer, Bryce, and Peter Giovacchini. *Psychoanalytic Treatment of
Characterological and Schizophrenic Disorders* (New York: Science House,
1967). In Chapter 4, "Office Treatment of Schizophrenic Patients: The
Use of Psychoanalytic Therapy with Few Parameters," Boyer describes
how he analyzed schizophrenics in his office without medication, in four
times weekly analysis and in a classical manner, that is by remaining
neutral and communicating through interpretation. Boyer and
Giovacchini collaborated over many years and, although both were
trained in ego psychology, their work with psychotic analysands led
them to follow a different path from that of many of their colleagues.
Both writers have been influenced by the work of Klein and Winnicott.
Their books represent the best example of the integration of ego
psychology and object relations theory.

Chiland, Colette. *Long-Term Treatments of Psychotic States* (New York:
Human Sciences Press, 1977). This book comprises fifty-four essays
derived from a symposium on psychosis, unique for its time because it
includes authors from around the world, with special representation of
French thinking. Harold Searles's response to an essay by Leopold
Bellak ends with a scathing critique of the trends toward drug
treatments in American society, claiming that these are a symptom
rather than a solution. Searles steadfastly refused to medicate any of his
schizophrenic patients when he worked at Chestnut Lodge in Rockville,
Maryland. There is an interesting contribution from the young Otto
Kernberg and a brief but moving address by Otto Will Jr. of Austen
Riggs. "In our view these disorders [schizophrenia] are paradigms of

human living, revealing in stark and disturbing clarity many of the ways of life that we impose on ourselves, destructive though they may be" (373).

Eigen, Michael. *The Psychotic Core* (Northvale and London: Jason Aronson, 1986). This is Eigen's best work, a highly original integration of Freud, Jung, Bion, and Winnicott on what constitutes psychosis. Chapter 3, "Mindlessness," will be of particular interest to readers of my text.

Garfield, David. *Unbearable Affect: A Guide to the Psychotherapy of Psychosis* (London: Karnac, 2009). This is perhaps the most readable work on schizophrenia to date, especially for those interested in the role of affects in its onset. Garfield invents a character—partly himself, partly a composite of colleagues—and, rather like my own text, takes the reader through the development of his own understanding of schizophrenia, based on the evolution of his career. Chapter 2, "Forms of Introduction: The Chief Complaint" (15–30), should be required reading. It gives crucial priority to taking a careful history of the background to the onset of schizophrenia. Chapter 3, "Psychotic Themes in the Precipitating Event" (31–44), is also highly relevant, especially Garfield's concept of "unlocking the precipitating event" (35). He seems to have been influenced by Elvin Semrad's seminars and those of his students in Boston, and he brings Semrad's brilliance to work with psychotic analysands. He is also deeply influenced by Heinz Kohut, and I think this is the best example yet of the level of clinical acumen that can be reached through that school's perspective. This book is accessible and can be read by anyone.

Garfield, David, and Daniel Mackler, editors. *Beyond Medication: Therapeutic Engagement and the Recovery from Psychosis* (London: Routledge, 2009). Garfield and Mackler have collected a group of contemporary psychoanalysts and psychotherapists, each tasked with discussing how to assess, engage, and facilitate change in the psychotic patient. This important book is wide ranging and also includes accounts by former schizophrenics.

Jackson, Murray, and Paul Williams. *Unimaginable Storms: A Search for Meaning in Psychosis* (London: Karnac, 1994). This is notable for the many transcripts of Jackson's work with paranoid schizophrenics and catatonic patients. These illustrate how, if one listens to what the patient says and seeks to find out what he means, this is intrinsically therapeutic. Jackson was a seminal figure at the Maudsley Hospital in London and has had a wide influence on the psychoanalytical treatment of psychotic people in the United Kingdom. A profound and highly original book.

Jung, Carl. *The Psychogenesis of Mental Disease*, in Collected Works of C. G. Jung, volume 3 (Princeton, N.J.: Princeton University Press, 1976). This classic text, reflecting Jung's early work with Eugen Bleuler at the Burghölzli Hospital in Zurich, is in many ways the finest example of Freudian psychoanalysis in the study of schizophrenia. Odd as this may seem, in that Jung and Freud are often considered to hold opposite views, Jung's thinking on schizophrenia is deeply derived from Freud's paradigms. Chapter 4, "Dementia Praecox and Hysteria," brilliantly illuminates the analytical theory of mental structure and illustrates remarkable depth of thought in the vital distinction between hysteria and schizophrenia. The collection ends with a broadcast on Voice of America (1956) where Jung concludes, "The investigation of schizophrenia is in my view one of the most important tasks for a psychiatry of the future" (255).

Karon, Bertram, and Gary VandenBos. *Psychotherapy of Schizophrenia: The Treatment of Choice* (Northvale and London: Jason Aronson, 1981). If the reader is a young psychoanalytical clinician, this is the book to read. It is a psychoanalytical textbook written by highly experienced and gifted psychoanalysts who have worked with many differing types of schizophrenics, including catatonic schizophrenics. The authors not only firmly believe in the efficacy of long-term psychotherapy, they are experienced in it. Of a catatonic schizophrenic who had been in hospital for five years and who rarely spoke except in single abrupt words, Karon writes: "What I learned from this patient was that even the most withdrawn of schizophrenic patients can be reached if the therapist is persistent and knowledgeable. Even though, in this case, the treatment at times reached heroic proportions—10 hours a day for 10 days with two therapists, before this patient uttered a single intelligible word—it was possible . . . to treat this patient successfully by psychotherapy" (2). I obviously share this view, although I have worked with only one catatonic schizophrenic (Megan), and my own work—determined purely by experience—was with younger schizophrenics who had not been in long-term hospitalization. Karon's optimism is shared by a team of analysts and clinicians in Quebec, known as GIVRIC, who have shown similar results. Talk to even catatonic schizophrenics who have been incarcerated for many years, and if you are prepared to put in the time they can be reached. For those who are understandably in some doubt about my own claims that intensive analysis can actually reverse a sudden onset of schizophrenia, here is Karon's conclusion about work with an incarcerated delinquent schizophrenic. "From this patient, I learned how quickly acute schizophrenic patients can remit and function nonpsychotically if they have not been previously subjected to mishandling. After a week of treatment (five sessions), this individual was no longer psychotic" (2). Jaws may have hit the ground upon reading such a claim, but I have found the same to be true in my own work—*if* the analyst receives the patient at the onset and before others have muddied the waters. The book provides a thorough introduction to the history of analytical views of schizophrenia, it takes a sympathetic view of the difficulties of the parents of schizophrenics, the clinical examples are clear and for the most part convincing (there is always a hazard in writing about schizophrenics that the writer can hystericise them so that sessions read as more dramatic than I think they actually are), and the writers address the role and function of countertransference in detail. The summary of their research, known as the Michigan State Psychotherapy Project, partly sponsored by the National Institute of Mental Health, is important reading for those who

value verification by a group rather than a text by a single author. The
book is currently out of print and one hopes it will be republished.

Lacan, Jacques. *The Psychoses* (Seminar Book 111, 1955–1956; London:
Routledge, 1993). Lacan's findings on the difference between neurotic
and psychotic structures. A brilliant work, but not for the timid of mind.

Laing, R. D. *The Divided Self: An Existential Study in Sanity and Madness*
(London: Tavistock, 1960). Laing's book changed the way
schizophrenics were viewed in Great Britain and in Europe. He
renounced both psychoanalytic and behavioral vocabularies and wrote
the book for the lay public, arguing that schizophrenia was—in
effect—a symptom of one's family life. A psychiatrist, Laing in this
work turned against the highly biased view held by most psychiatrists
that the only real schizophrenic was one who had to be in hospital. *The
Divided Self* inspired scores of psychiatrists to visit Laing in London,
where many remained and became an important part of his community,
especially the Philadelphia Association. Laing's clinical genius was his
endless patience and a quick wit—almost always imbued with profound
insight—that made him palatable to psychotic people. No other person
in the twentieth century did more to change the clinical view of
schizophrenia.

Leader, Darian. *What Is Madness?* (London: Hamish Hamilton, 2011). This
book is not, per se, about schizophrenia but it is included because
Leader's views of psychosis—like those of R. D. Laing—are
intelligently skeptical revisions of how and why we must reconsider our
notions of psychosis (or madness). This is also a work of remarkable
prose beauty and deeply inspiring.

Milner, Marion. *The Hands of the Living God: An Account of a Psycho-
Analytic Treatment* (London: Hogarth Press, 1969). Milner's account of
"Susan" is the most complete we have of the full analysis of someone
many would regard as schizophrenic. It is also the finest example of
work in the British Independent tradition. This is ecumenical and
pluralist, but above all it regards the analyst's struggle to understand

the analysand as a vivid part of any treatment. If there is any doubt
about the therapeutic efficacy of psychoanalytical work with the
psychotic analysand, this is the book to read. It is beautifully written,
hard to put down, and challenging in the best senses.

Pao, Ping-Nie. *Schizophrenic Disorders: Theory and Treatment from a
Psychodynamic Point of View* (New York: International Universities
Press, 1979). Pao was director of Chestnut Lodge in the 1970s, and this
book is a fine illustration of the influence of Harold Searles's thinking
on his colleagues. Part 4 of the book, on the psychotherapy of
schizophrenics, is full of clinical examples that concentrate on the
transformative effect of the analyst's empathic relation to his patient,
and the role of countertransference in working with psychosis.

Robbins, Michael. *Experiences of Schizophrenia: An Integration of the Personal,
Scientific, and Therapeutic* (New York: Guildford, 1993). At the time of its
publication this book was heralded by many senior figures in the
psychiatric and psychoanalytic community. The author skillfully
integrates many differing perspectives, offers extensive clinical examples,
and provides his own carefully constructed theory of psychic change in
the schizophrenic. It is, however, regrettable that this otherwise careful
writer diminishes his own work with sweeping categorical imperatives,
such as his assertion that it is not possible for schizophrenics to go through
extensive change "without the support of a mental hospital for some
substantial period of time" (271). As for clinicians who discuss work with
schizophrenics on an outpatient basis, according to Robbins, these
colleagues "are either not treating patients with schizophrenia" or they are
"subtly limiting the scope of the therapy" (271). These objections aside, it
is a valuable contribution to the literature.

Rosenfeld, David. *The Psychotic: Aspects of the Personality* (London:
Karnac, 1992). Typical among Argentinian psychoanalysts, Rosenfeld
has assimilated the British, French, and American literature on
psychosis, but he also includes here the brilliant work of South
American minds in this area, including Willy and Madeleine Baranger,

León Grinberg, Gregorio Klimovsky, and Heinrich Racker. Less a work on schizophrenia than a study of psychosis and the psychotic parts of the personality, this is an important contribution to the study of psychotic processes.

Rosenfeld, Herbert. *Psychotic States: A Psychoanalytical Approach* (London: Maresfield Reprints, 1985), and *Impasse and Interpretation* (London: Tavistock, 1987). If Searles is the figure with the greatest influence on the study and treatment of schizophrenia in the United States, then Herbert Rosenfeld is in a similar position in Great Britain. Rosenfeld links the psychotic parts of any self to the more specific psychotic areas of the various character disorders, and finally to schizophrenia. He thus illuminates the fact that schizophrenia is part of a spectrum. Like Milner, Rosenfeld provides many clinical examples of the way he works, in a classical Kleinian manner, simply by interpreting. These works are essential reading for any psychoanalyst working with psychotic analysands.

Schilder, Paul. *On Psychoses,* edited by Lauretta Bender (New York: International Universities Press, 1976). Schilder, one of Freud's pupils, was a pioneer in the study of schizophrenia and, although of interest primarily to scholars, his work is worth reviewing. Schilder's scope integrated the neuroscience of his time with psychological and biological factors in the formation of the schizophrenic. He was a polymath and referred in his essays to a wide variety of thinkers. He wrote, "Schizophrenic thinking is a continually moving drama" (318), and he distinguishes such thought processes from ordinary free association. His work has had a major impact on psychiatry and psychoanalysis, especially in the United States.

Searles, Harold. *Collected Papers on Schizophrenia and Related Subjects* (New York: International Universities Press, 1965). This is the best book by a psychoanalyst on schizophrenia, and it remains probably the most widely read text on the subject. Of particular note are Chapter 5, "The Psychodynamics of Vengefulness"; Chapter 8, "The Effort to Drive the

Other Person Crazy—An Element in the Aetiology and Psychotherapy
of Schizophrenia"; Chapter 13, "Schizophrenic Communication"; and
Chapter 21, "Scorn, Disillusionment, and Adoration in the
Psychotherapy of Schizophrenia." Searles (like Otto Will Jr. and Pao)
was at Chestnut Lodge, where he was influenced by the humane
approach of Frieda Fromm-Reichmann. He was also very familiar with
Independent Group thinking in Great Britain, with which he felt a
particular affinity. Above all else, however, he was an astonishingly gifted
clinician who shared many of his private thoughts and fantasies about his
patients in the interests of a certain kind of therapeutic honesty.

Sechehaye, Marguerite A. *Symbolic Realization: A New Method of
Psychotherapy Applied to a Case of Schizophrenia* (New York:
International Universities Press, 1951). This is one of the earliest
accounts of the successful treatment of a schizophrenic patient—
Renee—by one of the most gifted psychoanalysts of her time. The
book is compelling, offering unique views of what worked with Renee
and what did not. Sechehaye presented her work with Renee to a large
group of skeptical but supportive colleagues, who by the end of a
successful treatment abandoned their pessimism about how a
psychoanalytical therapy could recover a schizophrenic person. A
deeply moving book.

Silver, Ann-Louise, editor. *Psychoanalysis and Psychosis* (Madison:
International Universities Press, 1989). This is the best collection of
essays on the treatment of schizophrenia. Silver is one of the most
experienced psychoanalysts in the treatment of psychotic patients, having
worked at Chestnut Lodge for most of her career. She includes chapters
by such colleagues as Harold Searles, Joseph Smith, and Otto Allen Will
Jr. The book includes an essay by Martin Cooperman, "Defeating
Processes in Psychotherapy," that was required reading in its day.

Sullivan, Harry Stack. *Schizophrenia as a Human Process* (New York: Norton,
1962). This book collects Sullivan's essays on psychosis and schizophrenia
written primarily from the early 1920s to the late 1930s. Like many

Annotated Bibliography

American analysts, Sullivan writes like a pioneer in somewhat hostile surroundings. This gives his prose an edgy, caustic, and sometimes overly cryptic style. If he is not easy reading, this is also because he is forging a new way of thinking about schizophrenia as he goes along, and the book is full of brilliant and challenging insights, especially in Chapter 2, "Peculiarity of Thought in Schizophrenia" (26–99). Sullivan worked at Sheppard-Pratt (later called Sheppard Enoch Pratt) in Baltimore-Washington, where William Alanson White was the director. There he met and was analyzed by Clara Thompson, an analysand of Sándor Ferenczi. Sullivan's teachings and writing were disseminated throughout the world of psychiatry, becoming the foundation of interpersonal psychoanalysis. For Sullivan the connection between patient and analyst was crucial, and his chapter on the onset of schizophrenia, and the importance of attending to minute details, is very relevant to my own text and the idea of historicity. This is an invaluable book for clinicians.

Tustin, Frances. *Autism and Childhood Psychosis* (London: Science House, 1972). In this work, and in her many other subsequent publications, Tustin sets out the most intelligent and distinctive discussion of the dynamics of autism in children and of autistic features in the adult personality.

Volkan, Vamik. *Primitive Internalized Object Relations* (New York: International Universities Press, 1976). An important book that bridges ego psychology and object relations, with very clear clinical vignettes.

Index

Index

France, psychoanalysis training in, 57

Free association: as educational method, 48–49; Freud's development of, 1; and group mind, 53–54; and hallucinations, 49–50; in psychoanalysis, 69, 70, 71–72, 171, 172, 177; and self, 49, 51; therapeutic role of, 51–52; and unconscious thinking, 113

French psychoanalysis, 57

Freud, Anna, 25

Freud, Sigmund, 1–2, 3, 6, 7, 10, 55, 57, 117, 164, 170, 177, 206

Fromm-Reichmann, Frieda, 211

Frozen psychosis, 44–45

Garfield, David, 205

Gediman, Helen K., 203

Generative treatment, of schizophrenics, 8, 70, 78

Genocide, 162

Gestalts, 52

Giovacchini, Peter, 50, 204

González de Chávez, Manuel, 203

Gosling, Robert, 63

Green, André, 45

Grinberg, León, 210

Grotstein, James, 137

Group mind, 26, 53–54

Group process: Bion on, 62, 63, 64; of clinicians, 37; and collective mind, 54; complexity of, 162, 163; psychological forces implicit in, 161–62; and symbolic order, 161–64; and Tavi group, 63–64

Hallucinations: auditory, 88, 98, 146; and Bion's concept of "bizarre objects," 132, 200n1; compromises with, 83; daydreams as, 110; and free association, 49–50; negative hallucination, 45, 137; and oscillatory schizophrenics, 89; and psychoanalysis for schizophrenics, 5; schizophrenics' action defeating, 144; schizophrenics' disappearance from human world, 148; schizophrenics' experience of, 147; schizophrenics' explanation of, 145–46, 190, 192–94; and schizophrenics' formation of parallel universe, 172; and unconscious thinking, 122; visual, 47, 80, 88, 110, 146

Hallucinogens, 147

Hamburger, Michael, 119–20

Hamlet (Shakespeare), 6

Hearing and listening, 127–28, 131, 152

Hearing voices: friendly voices, 103–4, 105, 106, 140, 172, 196;

of functioning, 98–99, 100, 104,
108, 164; illusions of, 36–37; and
maternal order, 163–64, 165; and
metasexuality, 91, 99, 100;
parents' influence on, 160–61;
and somatoform expression, 152,
153, 164
Inner speech, 68, 103, 107, 114–17,
149, 159
Institute of Child Neuropsychiatry,
University of Rome, 125
Institute of Psychoanalysis,
London, 55–56
International Society for
Psychological and Social
Approaches to Psychosis
(ISPS), 3
Introjective identification, 129
Irish Republican Army, 59
Ironic relativism, 35

Jackson, Murray, 206
Jacobson, Roman, 118–19
James, William, 113
Joseph, Betty, 2
Jung, Carl, 52, 206

Karon, Bertram, 206–7
Kennedy, John F., 27, 28
Kennedy, Robert, 27, 28–29, 31
Kernberg, Otto, 204
Khan, Masud, 47, 144

King, Martin Luther, Jr., 27, 28,
29, 31
Klauber, John, 144
Klein, Melanie, 63, 200n1
Klimovsky, Gregorio, 210
Knowledge: assumed, 114, 115,
116; body, 123; unconscious,
90, 197
Kohut, Heinz, 205
Korea, 32

Lacan, Jacques, 57, 99–100,
161, 208
Laing, R. D., 2, 164, 203, 208
Language: alteration of ordinary
signifiers, 91, 165, 166, 182;
children's use of, 16–17, 111–15,
118; and concrete thinking, 130,
165; evading of, 143; linguistic
level of representation, 153;
private language, 149, 156, 165;
and schizophrenic poesis, 123;
sexualization of, 122; use of
android speech, 41, 43, 103, 176;
use of pronouns, 103, 111–15,
118, 119–20; and words that are
thinglike, 159, 166
Leader, Darian, 208
Lévi-Strauss, Claude, 57
Locke, John, 108
LSD, 3
Lucas, Richard, 68

Mackler, Daniel, 205
Madness, 36–37, 47
Mahler, Margaret, 17
Malcolm X, 27
Manic-depressive people, 50, 66
Marie Stopes Clinic, 59
Martindale, Brian, 3, 203
Maternal order, 163–64, 165
Meade, George Herbert, 113
Medications: for schizophrenics, 7,
  8, 50, 66, 67, 171, 187; in state
  mental institutions, 17
Memory, as mental faculty, 128–29,
  131–32
Mental faculties, schizophrenics'
  hiding of, 128–29, 131, 132, 172,
  174
Mental processes: schizophrenics'
  projection of, 133–34, 135, 136,
  138, 164; and TV mind, 136–37
Metasexuality: and elimination of
  duality of sexuality, 98; and
  hearing voices, 105, 106; as manic
  level solution, 99–100, 101, 102,
  106, 107; mystical union with
  inert objects, 91, 92, 97, 98–99,
  100, 101, 107; sexuality
  distinguished from, 133; sexuality
  subordinated in, 135
Milner, Marion, 208–9
Mind: complexity of, 4; creation of
  beta elements, 201n1; as group

process, 62, 63–64, 162;
  integrative work of, 88; ordinary
  axioms of, 181–82, 183, 184–86;
  preservation of, 140; and relation
  with self, 103, 196;
  schizophrenic's panic over loss
  of, 103; schizophrenics'
  projection of, 135, 136, 139, 141;
  signifying function of, 108; as
  synonymous with brain, 9. See
  also Collective mind; Group
  mind; Mental processes
Mindlessness, 123, 142, 147
Mourning, 77
Mozart, Wolfgang Amadeus, 66
My Lai massacre, 31
Mythological narrative, 80, 87–91,
  92, 170

Narcissists, 126
Narratives: children's stories,
  23–24, 25, 26, 50–51;
  mythological, 80, 87–91, 92, 170;
  narrative core of self, 170–71,
  176–77; and psychoanalysis for
  schizophrenics, 151–52
Negative hallucination, 45, 137
Non-psychotic functioning, 9
Normal people, 20, 37, 90, 163;
  psychotic areas of, 34;
  schizophrenics contrasted with,
  10, 34, 133, 197

Index

221

Self: acceptance of social order, 81;
in adolescence, 10; Bion on, 62,
63; body change as feature in
alteration of, 76; and
complexities of mind, 4;
derailment of, 178–79; in distinct
and acute onset of schizophrenia,
77, 78; distinction between "I"
and "me," 76, 113–15, 117, 119,
140, 141, 143, 169, 171; divided,
99, 181; embodied, 83; evolution
of, 25; false, 47, 96, 176; flooding
with unconscious thinking, 122;
fragmented, 69, 169, 171; and
free associations, 49, 51; function
of historicity, 88, 89, 114, 145,
170, 171; ideal, 47; as mechanical,
93, 94, 95; psychotic, 93, 185; and
relation with mind, 103, 196;
restoration of narrative core,
170–71, 176–77; robotic, 94; in
schizophrenic order, 81;
schizophrenics' hiding, 126–36,
143–44, 172; schizophrenics'
projection of "I," 104, 106,
140–41, 143, 169; schizophrenic's
safeguarding, 104, 164, 176;
schizophrenic's voices
originating from, 105–6, 107,
108, 109–10
Self-cure, 47
Self-fulfillment, 81

Self-idealizing action, 33
Self-therapy techniques, 47
Seminal signifiers, 52
Semrad, Elvin, 205
Senselessness, 141, 142, 144
Senses, 157, 165; schizophrenics'
hiding parts of self in objects,
126, 127, 135, 146; sensorial order,
182; and somatoforms, 150–52,
153, 154, 155, 156, 157–58, 159,
164, 165. *See also* Hearing voices;
Visual hallucinations
Sexuality: child's experience of
genital sexual excitement, 161; in
mad scenes, 36; schizophrenics'
nullifying reality of, 97, 99;
schizophrenics' projecting onto
objects, 132–35. *See also*
Metasexuality
Shakespeare, William, 6, 36
Sign system, 108
Silence: as communication, 144; loss
of vocalization, 149; in
psychoanalysis, 42, 63, 67, 69,
79, 128, 131, 143, 173, 175
Silver, Ann-Louise S., 203, 211
Size distortion, 80
Slow-onset schizophrenia, 75–76,
78–79
Small, S. Mouchley, 40
Smith, Joseph, 211
Social psychosis, 27

Sohn, Leslie, 2
Somatic liability, 158
Somatoform experience and
  representation, 152–55
Somatoforms: affective derivatives
  of, 158–59; expression of self's
  nascent experiences, 152, 153,
  157; moving from sensorial
  distress to speech, 154, 155–56;
  psychic toxins of new objects,
  150–51; schizophrenics'
  reading of, 153; and sensorial
  proprioceptive perception,
  164, 165; somatic irritants, 158;
  somatization of conflict,
  157–58
Sophocles, 36
Sound, sensitivity to, 75
Spinoza, Baruch, 57
State mental institutions, 17
Steiner, John, 2
Stephen, Adrian, 55
Stockbridge Institute of Nervous
  Disorders, 124
Strachey, Alix, 55
Strachey, James, 55
Structuralization, 185
Sullivan, Harry Stack, 211–12
Sullivan, Louis, 38
Symbol borrowing, 129
Symbolic equation, 131
Symbolic nodal points, 170

Symbolic order, 99, 132, 137; and
  group process, 161–64; and
  hearing voices, 110;
  schizophrenics' abandoning of,
  66, 143, 158–59, 182;
  schizophrenics' use of, 130–31,
  163, 164; verbal, 155–56
Syntactical agglomerations, 143, 165

Talking therapies, for
  schizophrenics, 8–10, 50, 170–71
Tausk, Victor, 16
Tavi group, 63–64
Tavistock Clinic, 35, 59, 62, 63–64,
  125
Tavistock Institute of Human
  Relations, 62
Thingness of things, 90–92, 104,
  120, 127, 143, 144
Thompson, Clara, 212
Thought: palimpsest of, 116–17;
  underlying logic of, 20
Thought processes: body gestures as
  means of expressing, 76;
  complexities of, 4; of manic-
  depressive people, 50; psychotic
  manifestations of, 151; of
  schizophrenic people, 68, 69, 73,
  74, 83; schizophrenics' acting out
  of, 126; schizophrenics' awareness
  of changes in, 79–80;
  schizophrenics' fear of telling

others, 75; schizophrenics'
reporting thoughts, 150;
schizophrenics' taking action to
block thoughts, 141–45, 147, 170,
172. *See also* Unconscious thinking
Trance-like state, 148
Tustin, Frances, 125, 212
TV mind, 136–37

"Unconscious Communication"
workshop, 51–52
Unconscious function: and free
association, 49, 50, 51, 52; of
metasexuality, 107; raw materials
of, 4; and Tavi group, 64
Unconscious knowledge, 90, 197
Unconscious perceptions, 165
Unconscious thinking: Blanchot on,
120–21; complexity of, 116–17,
120; as core axiom of depth
psychology, 116; exercise of, 53;
and free association, 113; relation
to consciousness, 122–23, 146, 183,
184, 185; schizophrenic child's
lack of barrier between conscious
and unconscious thought, 121–22;
talking therapies promoting, 9
University College Hospital,
London, 59
University of Buffalo, 38–39,
48–49; student health center,
39–45, 53

University of London, 59
University of Rome, 125

Valium, 7
VandenBos, Gary, 206–7
Vegetative state, 132
Vietnam War, 27, 29, 31, 32, 38
Violence: children's reactions to,
29, 31, 118; in mad scenes, 36;
and psychotic personalities,
41–44, 47
Visual hallucinations, 47, 80, 88,
110, 146
Vocalization, loss of, 149
Voice of God, 141
Volkan, Vamik, 212
Vygotsky, Lev, 116

War, 162
Westmoreland, William C., 31
White, William Alanson, 212
Will, Otto, Jr., 204, 211
Williams, Paul, 206
Winnicott, D. W., 25, 35–36, 47, 56,
144, 157
Woolf, Virginia, 55
World War II, 31, 32
Wright, Frank Lloyd, 38

Yeats, W. B., 74, 196, 197
Yippie movement, 28